323.1
Tac

27.50

The Civil Rights Movement

JAMES TACKACH

[OPPOSING
VIEWPOINTS®
DIGESTS]

WITHDRAWN

Greenhaven Press, Inc., San Diego, California

Library of Congress Cataloging-in-Publication Data

Tackach, James
     The civil rights movement / by James Tackach
        p.   cm. — (Opposing viewpoints digests)
     Includes bibliographical references and index.
     ISBN 0-7377-0355-5 (pbk. : alk. paper) —
     ISBN 0-7377-0356-3 (lib. : alk. paper)
     1. Afro-Americans—Civil rights—History—20th century—
Juvenile literature. 2. Civil rights movements—United States—
History—20th century—Juvenile literature. [1. Afro-Americans—
Civil rights—History—20th century. 2. Civil rights movements—
History—20th century. 3. Race relations.] I. Title. II. Series.
     E185.61 .T17   2001
323.1'196073—dc21   00-12122

Cover Photo: AP Photo/Matt Herron/Smithsonian
American Stock/Archive Photos: 32
Library of Congress: 9, 13, 15, 52, 68, 76
Schomburg Center for Research in Black Culture: 22

© 2001 by Greenhaven Press, Inc.
PO Box 289009, San Diego, CA 92198-9009

Printed in the U.S.A.

CONTENTS

FOREWORD

The only way in which a human being can make some approach to knowing the whole of a subject is by hearing what can be said about it by persons of every variety of opinion and studying all modes in which it can be looked at by every character of mind. No wise man ever acquired his wisdom in any mode but this.

—John Stuart Mill

Greenhaven Press's Opposing Viewpoints Digests in history are designed to aid in examining important historical issues in a way that develops critical thinking and evaluating skills. Each book presents thought-provoking argument and stimulating debate on a single topic. In analyzing issues through opposing views, students gain a social and historical context that cannot be discovered in textbooks. Excerpts from primary sources reveal the personal, political, and economic side of historical topics such as the American Revolution, the Great Depression, and the Bill of Rights. Students begin to understand that history is not a dry recounting of facts, but a record founded on ideas—ideas that become manifest through lively discussion and debate. Digests immerse students in contemporary discussions: Why did many colonists oppose a bill of rights? What was the original intent of the New Deal and on what grounds was it criticized? These arguments provide a foundation for students to assess today's debates on censorship, welfare, and other issues. For example, *The Great Depression: Opposing Viewpoints Digests* offers opposing arguments on controversial issues of the time as well as views and interpretations that interest modern historians. A major debate during Franklin D. Roosevelt's administration was whether the president's New Deal programs would lead to a permanent welfare state, creating a citizenry dependent on government money. *The Great Depression* covers this issue from both historical and modern perspectives, allowing students to critically evaluate arguments both in the context of their time and through the benefit of historical hindsight.

This emphasis on debate makes Digests a useful tool for writing reports, research papers, and persuasive essays. In addition to supplying students with a range of possible topics and supporting material, the Opposing Viewpoints Digests offer unique features through which young readers acquire and sharpen critical thinking and reading skills. To assure an appropriate and consistent reading level for young adults, all essays in each volume are written by a single author. Each essay heavily quotes readable primary sources that are fully cited to allow for further research and documentation. Thus, primary sources are introduced in a context to enhance comprehension.

In addition, each volume includes extensive research tools, including a section comprising excerpts from original documents pertaining to the issue under discussion. In *The Bill of Rights*, for example, readers can examine the English Magna Carta, the Virginia State Bill of Rights drawn up in 1776, and various opinions by U.S. Supreme Court justices in key civil rights cases, as well as an unabridged version of the U.S. Bill of Rights. These documents both complement the text and give students access to a wide variety of relevant sources in a single volume. Additionally, a "facts about" section allows students to peruse facts and statistics that pertain to the topic. These statistics are also fully cited, allowing students to question and analyze the credibility of the source. Two bibliographies, one for young adults and one listing the author's sources, are also included; both are annotated to guide student research. Finally, a comprehensive index allows students to scan and locate content efficiently.

Greenhaven's Opposing Viewpoints Digests, like Greenhaven's higher level and critically acclaimed Opposing Viewpoints Series, have been developed around the concept that an awareness and appreciation for the complexity of seemingly simple issues is particularly important in a democratic society. In a democracy, the common good is often, and very appropriately, decided by open debate of widely varying views. As one of democracy's greatest advocates, Thomas Jefferson, observed, "Difference of opinion leads to inquiry, and inquiry to truth." It is to this principle that Opposing Viewpoints Digests are dedicated.

The Movement to End Racial Segregation and Discrimination in America

The Civil War and the Thirteenth Amendment to the U.S. Constitution, enacted in 1865, several months after the war's close, ended American slavery. Despite slavery's disappearance, however, the United States remained divided over racial issues for another century. Congress amended the Constitution twice more during the five years following the war in an attempt to extend full citizenship rights to freed slaves and their descendants. The Fourteenth Amendment, enacted in 1868, guaranteed "equal protection of the laws" to all U.S. citizens; the Fifteenth Amendment, adopted in 1870, prohibited any state from denying citizens the right to vote "on account of race, color, or previous condition of servitude." Despite the passage of these two amendments, neighborhoods, schools, businesses, and social gathering places in the Southern states remained rigidly segregated along racial lines for almost a century. In the North, racial segregation became less overt, but African Americans still encountered discrimination when they applied for jobs and searched for housing.

The civil rights movement was a large-scale protest movement waged to eliminate the racial divisions in American society. Historians have placed the beginnings of that movement in the years following World War II. The movement lasted through the late 1960s, when the last important pieces of civil rights legislation became law and when Martin Luther King Jr., the recognized leader of the civil rights movement, was killed by an assassin's bullet. The roots of the civil rights movement, however, extend to the years following the Civil War.

The Era of Jim Crow

Despite the passage of the Fourteenth and Fifteenth Amendments, lawmakers and citizens throughout the South attempted to keep African Americans in an inferior position in post–Civil War Southern society. In 1866, Nathan Bedford Forrest of Tennessee, an ex-Confederate general, formed the Ku Klux Klan, a paramilitary force whose main function was to intimidate African American citizens who attempted to vote or exercise other constitutional rights. Southern state legislatures and city councils enacted legislation designed to segregate Southern society along racial lines. Laws were passed preventing African Americans from living in certain areas, lodging in certain hotels, eating in certain restaurants, traveling in the same train cars as whites, and seeking employment in certain professions. If black citizens were arrested for some legal transgression, they faced an unfair trial by an all-white jury and a stiff prison sentence. These legal measures, enacted in reaction to the passage of the Fourteenth and Fifteenth Amendments, became known as the Jim Crow laws, named for a black character who often appeared in African American minstrel shows.

In 1896, the Jim Crow laws received the blessing of the U.S. Supreme Court in the case of *Plessy v. Ferguson*. Homer Plessy, an African American from Louisiana, had been arrested and fined for traveling in a whites-only train car. He appealed his fine to the Supreme Court, but the Court ruled against Plessy, by a 7–1 vote. Associate Justice Henry Billings

Brown, delivering the Court's opinion, stated that the Four-teenth Amendment was not designed to eliminate all legal distinctions based on race and color: "If one race be inferior to the other socially, the Constitution of the United States cannot put them upon the same plane."[1]

Early Civil Rights Activists

Voices of protest rose from the African American community while the South was erecting its Jim Crow society. Frederick Douglass, a former slave who had played a dramatic role in the effort to rid America of slavery, continued to agitate for civil rights for African Americans after the Civil War. Douglass died in 1895, the year that W.E.B. Du Bois received a Ph.D. from Harvard University. Du Bois became a university professor and gained fame for his essays on American race relations. In 1903, Du Bois published several of his essays in book form under the title *The Souls of Black Folk*. The opening paragraph of Du Bois's book boldly asserted that "the problem of the Twentieth Century is the problem of the color-line."[2] Du Bois demanded the right to vote, civic equality, and quality education for African Americans.

In 1909, Du Bois formed the National Association for the Advancement of Colored People (NAACP) to work to establish equal citizenship rights for all American citizens. *Crisis*, the NAACP's monthly journal, edited by Du Bois, featured articles on racial and civil rights issues by prominent black and white writers.

Slow Progress

Despite the efforts of Du Bois and his followers, progress on civil rights was slow during the first half of the twentieth century. In the South, racial barriers remained firmly in place, upheld by both law and custom. Black citizens were prohibited from voting. Those who demanded their civil rights were intimidated with force. They were fired from their jobs; their homes were burned; in the worst cases, they were beaten and lynched. During the opening decades of the twentieth cen-

Despite the efforts of the National Association for the Advancement of Colored People, progress on civil rights was slow.

tury, hundreds of thousands of Southern blacks migrated to the North, where they hoped for a better life. In the North, however, African Americans fared only marginally better. They lived in rigidly segregated neighborhoods. They toiled at low-paying jobs. Many lacked access to quality schooling.

Segregation and racial discrimination had become a national problem in a nation whose Declaration of Independence and Constitution asserted the equality of all citizens. Walter White, an NAACP officer, put the problem into focus in a speech in July 1930: "Unless disfranchisement, arbitrary residential segregation, lynching, unequal apportionment of school funds, injustice in the courts, Jim Crowism, and the other evils which are foisted upon Negroes in parts of the United States can be ended, then democracy itself fails in the United States."[3]

A Movement's Beginnings

In 1933, Thurgood Marshall graduated from the Howard University School of Law and joined the NAACP as an attorney. Marshall earnestly began work on legal cases involving the civil rights of African Americans. In 1936, he won a lawsuit on behalf of nine African American students who had been denied admission to the University of Maryland School of Law because of their race. Two years later, Marshall won a similar case in Missouri.

In 1941, A. Philip Randolph, a labor organizer and civil rights activist, planned a march on Washington to demand more and better jobs for African Americans in the defense industry. President Franklin Roosevelt reacted by issuing an executive order prohibiting employment discrimination in any company dealing with defense contracts and by forming the Fair Employment Practices Committee.

World War II

In 1941, the United States went to war against Nazi Germany, and Americans of all races united behind the effort to defeat Adolf Hitler's racist regime. Thousands of African American soldiers, sailors, airmen, and nurses took part in this conflict, but they returned from the war to an American society still sharply divided along racial lines. Constance Baker Motley, an NAACP attorney, articulated what many returning African American war veterans felt as they returned to the United States after serving in the military:

> I think people became more aware that something had to be done about the fact that black servicemen were overseas dying for this country, and . . . they would be coming home to a situation that said, in effect, You're a second-class citizen. You can't go to school with white children, or your children can't. You can't stay in a hotel or eat in a restaurant because you're black. And I think that gave momentum, particularly in the black community, for what became the civil rights movement of the 1950s and 1960s.[4]

Shortly after the war ended, the Brooklyn Dodgers baseball team signed a flashy infielder from the Kansas City Monarchs of the Negro League. In 1947, after playing for two years on Dodger minor league teams, Jackie Robinson made his major league debut, becoming the first African American major league player. The next year, President Harry Truman ordered the integration of the U.S. armed forces. Previously, black and white servicemen had served in separate battalions. That same year, Truman asked Congress to enact civil rights legislation to erase racial discrimination, asserting that "Our national government must show the way."[5]

Brown v. Board of Education

The event that gave the civil rights movement its initial momentum was a Supreme Court decision in a case concerning segregated public schools. Martin Luther King Jr. later referred to the decision as "an exit sign that suddenly appeared to one who had walked through a long and desolate corridor, . . . a way out of the darkness of segregation."[6]

Between 1949 and 1951, the NAACP had filed five lawsuits concerning segregated public schools. NAACP attorneys, led by Thurgood Marshall, argued that segregated schools violated the equal protection clause of the Fourteenth Amendment, because black schoolchildren were receiving an inferior education. Those cases found their way to the Supreme Court, and in May 1954, the Court issued its unanimous decision in those cases under the umbrella title *Brown v. Board of Education of Topeka, Kansas.*

Chief Justice Earl Warren's written opinion asserted that segregated schools damage black students by generating "a feeling of inferiority as to their status in the community that may affect their hearts and minds in a way unlikely ever to be undone." The Court ruled that "in the field of public education the doctrine of 'separate but equal' has no place. Separate educational facilities are inherently unequal."[7]

Predictably, the *Brown* decision was condemned in the South and applauded in the North. Governor Henry Talmadge of Georgia asserted that the Supreme Court "has reduced the Constitution to a mere scrap of paper."[8] An editorial in the *Newark* (New Jersey) *Star-Ledger* called the *Brown* decision "one of the most important developments in the touchy problem of race relations since the emancipation of the slaves during the Civil War."[9]

Although the Warren court's decision focused only on segregated schools, lower courts began striking down other segregation laws, citing the *Brown* case as a precedent. For example, a year after the *Brown* decision, a U.S. district court ruled that the city of Baltimore could no longer segregate its public beaches or parks. That same year, the Supreme Court invalidated a law that segregated public golf courses in Atlanta. In a speech delivered in 1957, Martin Luther King Jr. stated that with the *Brown* decision, "we could gradually see the old order of segregation and discrimination passing away, and a new order of freedom and justice coming into being."[10]

The Montgomery Bus Boycott

King would test the reaches of the *Brown* decision eighteen months after it was issued in Montgomery, Alabama, where the twenty-six-year-old King served as a Baptist minister. King's targets were segregated public buses. On December 1, 1955, Rosa Parks, an African American seamstress who served the local chapter of the NAACP as a secretary, was arrested and fined for refusing to surrender her bus seat to a white passenger. King and other leaders in Montgomery's African American community met and decided to boycott the city's buses until Montgomery's segregated seating law was repealed.

The Montgomery bus boycott lasted more than a year. African American citizens walked to work, carpooled, bicycled, and took taxis operated by black cabbies. The nation took note of the firm resolve of the Montgomery protesters. On December 20, 1956, the Supreme Court ordered Montgomery to end segregated seating on its municipal buses. King and his followers had scored a major victory in their struggle for civil rights.

A Montgomery, Alabama, police officer fingerprints Rosa Parks after her arrest for refusing to surrender her seat on a bus to a white person.

A Movement Gains Momentum

Writing about the Montgomery bus boycott, historian Harvard Sitkoff states, "Not since the Civil War had the Southern black rank-and-file protested so visibly and volubly for equality. Their numbers and courage would point the way for countless other blacks to assert their rights militantly."[11]

Shortly after his victory in Montgomery, King formed the Southern Christian Leadership Conference, which would work to end racial segregation and discrimination throughout the United States. In 1957, Congress responded to King's call for civil rights by passing the first important piece of civil rights legislation since the Reconstruction Era that followed Civil War. The Civil Rights Act of 1957 established a civil rights division in the U.S. Justice Department and prescribed punishments for anyone restricting a citizen's right to vote.

School Desegregation Battles

Some of the most bitter civil rights battles took place in the nation's public schools. Three years after the *Brown* decision, most Southern schools remained segregated. In 1957, the school board in Little Rock, Arkansas, ordered the city's high school integrated on a limited basis—nine black students were to enroll in Central High in September. On the first day of class, these nine students encountered a mob of angry students and 250 Arkansas National Guardsmen, ordered by Governor Orval Faubus to block the integration of Central High. For three weeks, with the entire nation following the event, the African American students attempted to attend classes but were turned away by Guardsmen and white protesters. Finally, on September 24, President Dwight Eisenhower, asserting that a court's orders "cannot be flouted with impunity by an individual or mob of extremists,"[12] ordered federal troops, the 101st Airborne Division, to escort the nine students to class. Central High School became integrated.

A similar crisis occurred in 1962 when James Meredith, an African American Mississippian and air force veteran, attempted to enroll at the all-white University of Mississippi. Meredith was turned down on account of his race. A U.S. court of appeals, citing the *Brown* decision, ordered the University of Mississippi to admit Meredith, but Governor Ross Barnett blocked Meredith's registration. After President John Kennedy pressured Barnett to change his stand, an angry mob prevented Meredith from registering. A riot broke out on campus, during which two people were killed.

On September 30, President Kennedy addressed the nation on the crisis in Mississippi. "Americans are free . . . to disagree with the law but not to disobey it," he stated. "For in a government of laws and not of men, no man . . . and no mob . . . is entitled to defy a court of law."[13] The next day, Meredith, protected by three hundred federal marshals, began attending classes.

In 1962 James Meredith (center) sued for the right to enroll in the University of Mississippi and won.

Nonviolent Protests

King insisted that any protests over civil rights must be non-violent; in a 1966 speech, he asserted that "violence, even in self-defense, creates more problems than it solves."[14] Hence, his favored weapons of combat were the boycott, sit-in, and protest march. The boycott had worked successfully in Montgomery. In February 1960, African American college students began a series of sit-ins in a whites-only Woolworth's lunch counter in Greensboro, North Carolina. These students, later joined by white students, sat calmly at the segregated lunch counter and waited to be served. White patrons insulted them, threatened them, and poured sugar and soft drinks on their heads. The police arrested them for trespassing. But within two weeks, the restaurant sit-in movement spread to eleven other Southern cities. Over the next three months, restaurant chains across the South began announcing an end to segregated service.

The civil rights movement gained energy from massive protest marches, the two most important occurring in Washington, D.C., in 1963 and in Alabama in 1965. At the end of August 1963, King's Southern Christian Leadership Conference and other civil rights groups sponsored a March on Washington for Jobs and Freedom. More than 250,000 protesters descended on Washington and gathered at the Lincoln Memorial for a civil rights rally. The keynote speaker was King, who delivered his most famous speech, "I Have a Dream," in the style of a sermon. After criticizing his nation for its racism, King boldly asserted that he had a dream for a better America: "I still have a dream. It is a dream deeply rooted in the American dream that one day this nation will rise up and live out the true meaning of its creed—we hold these truths to be self-evident, that all men are created equal." [15]

In March 1965, King led a fifty-mile march from Selma to Montgomery, Alabama, to protest that state's efforts to prevent black citizens from voting. The marchers reached their goal despite intimidation by Ku Klux Klansmen, angry whites, and local law enforcement officials. At the conclusion of the march, King delivered a speech in which he announced that "segregation was on its deathbed in Alabama" and that he and his followers would "march on ballot boxes until all over Alabama God's children will be able to walk the earth in decency and honor." [16]

Key Legislation

These two famous protest marches led directly to the passage of the most important pieces of civil rights legislation during the civil rights movement. In the wake of the March on Washington for Jobs and Freedom, Congress began a long and bitter debate on a civil rights bill that would outlaw discrimination in employment and in restaurants, hotels, sports arenas, and other social gathering places. The Civil Rights Act of 1964 finally became law on July 2, 1964, signed by President Lyndon Johnson, who called the bill "a challenge . . . to eliminate the last vestiges of injustice in our beloved country." [17]

The Selma-to-Montgomery march resulted in the passage, in August 1965, of the Voting Rights Act, which outlawed literacy tests and other tactics implemented to keep African Americans from voting in the South. In signing the bill into law, President Johnson called the act "a victory for the freedom of the American Negro" and "also a victory for the freedom of the American nation."[18]

A Bloody Conclusion

Despite this landmark legislation, many African Americans were frustrated by the nation's slow progress on civil rights. That frustration erupted into violence in Watts, California, in 1965 and in Detroit, Michigan, and in Newark, New Jersey, in 1967. In 1968, King was murdered in Memphis, Tennessee, while organizing a rally to support striking sanitation workers. Riots in several U.S. cities followed King's death, which, many historians suggest, ended the civil rights movement. King's message of racial integration was silenced by more radical African American leaders who embraced "Black Power" as their motto. Some of these leaders, such as Elijah Muhammad and Malcolm X of the Nation of Islam, argued for a separate black state within the United States.

Although the civil rights movement may have ended with King's death, some of its energy and spirit endured. During and after the civil rights movement, other minorities within the United States became more forceful in demanding their civil rights. During the last quarter of the twentieth century, women, homosexuals, Latinos, Asian Americans, and other groups asserted their right to enjoy the rights and privileges of U.S. citizenship. Congress, state legislatures, and city and town councils across the country reacted by enacting legislation and policies whose goal was to erase discrimination based on race, ethnicity, religion, gender, and sexual orientation. Professions previously closed to women and racial minorities, either by policy or by custom, opened themselves to accommodate these groups. Many corporations and educational institutions put in place affirmative action policies—plans designed to integrate workplaces by actively recruiting and promoting women and ethnic minorities.

Although historians continue to debate the long-term achievements of the civil rights movement, few would argue that the movement left the United States unchanged. Discrimination sanctioned by law virtually vanished from the American landscape. American government, workplaces, and communities became more integrated. In terms of race, the United States of 1950 and the United States of 2000 are two very different nations.

1. Quoted in Otto H. Olsen, ed., *The Thin Disguise: Turning Point in Negro History*, Plessy v. Ferguson. New York: Humanities Press, 1967, p. 112.

2. W.E.B. Du Bois, *The Souls of Black Folk*. New York: Penguin Books, 1989, p. 1.

3. Quoted in Sanford Wexler, *The Civil Rights Movement: An Eyewitness History*. New York: Facts On File, 1993, p. 26.

4. Quoted in Henry Hampton and Steve Fayer, *Voices of Freedom: An Oral History of the Civil Rights Movement from the 1950s Through the 1980s*. New York: Bantam Books, 1990, p. xxv.

5. Quoted in Wexler, *The Civil Rights Movement*, p. 27.

6. Martin Luther King Jr., *I Have a Dream: Writings and Speeches That Changed the World*. San Francisco: HarperSanFrancisco, 1992, p. 65.

7. Quoted in Wexler, *The Civil Rights Movement*, pp. 275–76.

8. Quoted in Wexler, *The Civil Rights Movement*, p. 47.

9. Quoted in Wexler, *The Civil Rights Movement*, p. 49.

10. King, *I Have a Dream*, p. 19.

11. Harvard Sitkoff, *The Struggle for Black Equality 1954–1980*. New York: Hill and Wang, 1981, p. 58.

12. Quoted in Wexler, *The Civil Rights Movement*, p. 92.

13. Quoted in Wexler, *The Civil Rights Movement*, p. 155.

14. King, *I Have a Dream*, p. 130.

15. King, *I Have a Dream*, p. 104.

16. King, *I Have a Dream*, pp. 122–23.

17. Quoted in Wexler, *The Civil Rights Movement*, p. 210.

18. Quoted in Wexler, *The Civil Rights Movement*, p. 242.

CHAPTER 1

The Need for a Civil Rights Movement

"The problem of the Twentieth Century is the problem of the color-line."

American Negroes Are Treated as Second-Class Citizens

Author's note: This viewpoint is written from a mid-1950s perspective.

A decade has passed since the United States and its allies defeated the racist regime of Adolf Hitler in the Second World War. People all over the world were properly appalled when Hitler's crimes against the Jewish people became apparent. Millions were sent to their deaths in concentration camps. Their properties were confiscated, their businesses destroyed or taken over by government authorities.

After learning of Hitler's atrocities, many Americans began to look with a critical eye on their own country's treatment of its minority citizens. Does America treat its Negroes as Hitler treated Germany's Jews? Certainly American Negroes are not being herded into concentration camps to await execution. Still, any American who honestly examines the plight of America's Negroes must conclude that they are treated as second-class citizens.

Segregation and Discrimination

A half-century ago, W.E.B. Du Bois, the great Negro professor and author, asserted that "the problem of the Twentieth

Century is the problem of the color-line."[1] Today, in many areas of the United States, Negroes still face both segregation and discrimination. Throughout the South, Negroes are prohibited by law and custom from engaging in daily activities that most Americans undertake without interference. In many places a Negro cannot sit at a lunch counter and order a meal or take a room at a hotel or motel. A Negro woman cannot take her children to a public beach, and her husband cannot play a round of golf on a public golf course. In many municipalities throughout the nation, Negro passengers must sit in the rear section of a bus, and they must surrender their seats to white passengers when the bus fills. Many institutions of higher learning are closed to Negroes, as are the professions that require college degrees. When a Negro couple searches for a place to live, they are informed that certain sections of town are off limits to them, even if they can afford to pay the rent.

Would white Americans accept living under these conditions without protest? As Benjamin E. Mays, president of Morehouse College in Atlanta, recently stated, "Segregation is immoral because it has inflicted a wound upon the soul of the segregated and so restricted his mind that millions of Negroes now alive will never be cured of the disease of inferiority."[2]

Segregated Schools

Negro children learn of their second-class status at an early age. In many states, public schools are still racially segregated; white children attend one school, while the Negro children of the same city or town attend another school. And rarely are the schools of equal quality. The school for white students is almost always better equipped; its teachers are of a higher quality; and its building and grounds are in better repair.

In the recent Supreme Court decision of *Brown v. Board of Education of Topeka, Kansas,* the high court asserted that Negro children who attend segregated schools begin to see themselves as second-class citizens: "To separate them [Negro students] from others of similar age and qualifications solely because of

Forced to attend segregated schools which were poorly equipped and in disrepair, Negro children learned from an early age that society viewed them as second-class citizens.

their race generates a feeling of inferiority as to their status in the community that may affect their hearts and minds in a way unlikely ever to be undone."[3] These children grow up viewing themselves as undeserving of their civil rights.

Unequal Protection of the Law

The Fourteenth Amendment to the U.S. Constitution guarantees all citizens "equal protection of the law," but that constitutional guarantee is rarely applied to Negroes. Since the Civil War, thousands of Negroes accused of crimes—many falsely accused—have been lynched without a trial. Twice during the 1930s, the House of Representatives passed antilynching bills, but senators from the South killed both bills before they became law. Negroes who do receive trials are often convicted on flimsy evidence by all-white juries.

The constitutional right to vote, guaranteed by the Fifteenth and Nineteenth Amendments, is often denied to col-

ored citizens. In the South, less than one-fourth of Negro citizens qualified to vote are registered to cast a ballot. Literacy
tests, poll taxes, and various means of intimidation prevent
Southern Negroes from registering to vote and from voting.
Ira Mosley, a Negro schoolteacher writing in the *St. Louis Dis-
patch* in 1949, stated, "The right to vote is basic. At least one
Negro was lynched last year solely on the ground that he was
trying to exercise his right."[4]

Problems in the North

Segregation and discrimination against the Negro are not
limited to the South. In the North, segregation and discrimination are less overt but still apparent. A high percentage of
Northern Negroes live in the slums of the nation's large
cities—New York, Detroit, Chicago, and Philadelphia. Housing is substandard; neighborhoods are infested with crime and
drugs; and good jobs are difficult to find. In a recent essay,
James Baldwin, the talented Negro essayist from Harlem, described the conditions under which many of the North's Negroes live:

> Harlem, physically at least, has changed very little in
> my parents' lifetime or in mine. Now as then the build-
> ings are old and in desperate need of repair, the streets
> are crowded and dirty, there are too many human be-
> ings per square block. Rents are 10 to 58 per cent
> higher than anywhere else in the city; food, expensive
> everywhere, is more expensive here and of an inferior
> quality; and now that the war is over and money is
> dwindling, clothes are carefully shopped for and sel-
> dom bought. Negroes, traditionally the last to be hired
> and the first to be fired, are finding jobs harder to get,
> and, while prices are rising implacably, wages are going
> down. . . .
>
> All of Harlem is pervaded by a sense of congestion,
> rather like the insistent, maddening, claustrophobic

pounding in the skull that comes from trying to breathe in a very small room with all the windows shut.[5]

The Northern Negro is only marginally better off than his Southern counterpart. In a thriving postwar economy, the Negro lags far behind the white American. His living environment, education, and job are all second-class.

A Call to Action

All Americans, white and colored, must work to end segregation and discrimination and thereby allow the Negro an equal position in American society. All Americans should embrace the position articulated a few years ago by the Southern Regional Council, a racially integrated organization working for social reform and economic development in the South:

> The South of the future, toward which our efforts are directed, is a South freed of the stultifying inheritances from the past. It is a South where the measure of a man will be his ability, not his race; where a common citizenship will work in democratic understanding for a common good; where all who labor will be rewarded in proportion to their skill and achievement; where all can feel confident of personal safety and equality before the law; where there will exist no double standard in housing, health, education, or other public services; where segregation will be recognized as a cruel and needless penalty on the human spirit, and will no longer be imposed; where, above all, every individual will enjoy a full share of dignity and self-respect, in recognition of his creation in the image of God.[6]

The Supreme Court, in its *Brown v. Board of Education* decision, opened the way for the creation of a new, thoroughly integrated nation, a nation in which no American will be treated as a second-class citizen.

1. W.E.B. Du Bois, *The Souls of Black Folk.* New York: Penguin Books, 1989, p. 1.

2. Quoted in William Dudley, ed., *The Civil Rights Movement: Opposing Viewpoints.* San Diego: Greenhaven Press, 1996, p. 85.

3. Quoted in Sanford Wexler, *The Civil Rights Movement: An Eyewitness History.* New York: Facts On File, 1993, pp. 275–76.

4. Quoted in Wexler, *The Civil Rights Movement,* p. 27.

5. James Baldwin, *Notes of a Native Son.* Boston: Beacon Press, 1955, p. 57.

6. Quoted in John Egerton, *Speak Now Against the Day: The Generation Before the Civil Rights Movement in the South.* New York: Alfred A. Knopf, 1995, p. 565.

"The Negroes of the U.S.A. are today by far the most fortunate members of their race to be found anywhere on earth."

American Negroes Are Not Treated as Second-Class Citizens

Author's note: This viewpoint is written from a mid-1950s perspective.

A decade after winning the second great world war waged to save the world from tyranny, the United States is experiencing a period of extraordinary economic and social progress. The booming American economy is creating new jobs. New consumer products like the television, refrigerator, and washing machine—easily affordable for millions of Americans—are finding their way into American homes. More American youths are graduating from high school—and attending college—than ever before. Today's Americans are eating better, living in better homes, and receiving better medical care than Americans of any previous generation.

Amid this unprecedented progress and prosperity, however, a handful of social critics and agitators are determined to paint a negative picture of life in the United States. Their target is the American Negro, whom, they claim, is being treated as a second-class citizen. An honest look at the life of the American Negro, however, will reveal that he, too, is experiencing the same unprecedented social and economic progress enjoyed by other Americans.

The Most Fortunate Members of Their Race

First, it must be said that American Negroes live in better conditions than Negroes in other parts of the world, a point expressed by historian Herbert Ravenel Sass in a recent article in *Atlantic Monthly*:

> It must be realized that the Negroes of the U.S.A. are today by far the most fortunate members of their race to be found anywhere on earth. Instead of being the hapless victim of unprecedented oppression, it is nearer the truth that the Negro in the United States is by and large the product of friendliness and helpfulness unequaled in any comparable instance in all history. Nowhere else in the world, at any time of which there is record, has a helpless, backward people of another color been so swiftly uplifted and so greatly benefited by a dominant race.[1]

In Africa and in other parts of the world, millions of Negroes live in desperate poverty. They lack nutritious food on a daily basis; they lack medical care; and they receive no formal education.

A Decade of Progress

Facts and statistics tell the story of a decade of steady economic and social progress for America's Negroes. For example, from 1947 through 1952, the median Negro-family yearly income rose from $1,614 to $2,338. In 1940, the average life span of an American Negro was 53.1 years; by 1953, that average had risen to 61.7 years. Since the beginning of World War II, twelve states and more than thirty cities have enacted fair-employment laws to ensure that Negroes can find suitable jobs.

In the recent *Brown v. Board of Education* decision, the U.S. Supreme Court stated that the South's segregated schools were of an inferior quality. The Court's opinion notwithstanding, educational opportunities are increasing for the American Negro. In 1930, only 60 percent of Negroes between the ages of five and nineteen attended school; today, that number is more than 75 percent. Many states have opened colleges and universities specifically designed to educate Negro youths. Jackson State College in Mississippi, Morehouse College and Spelman College in Atlanta, Howard University in Washington, and Meharry Medical College in Nashville are just a handful of the many quality institutions of higher learning where an academically qualified Negro student can obtain a college or graduate degree.

Even W.E.B. Du Bois, the Negro educator and social activist, conceded in a journal article several years ago that the status of the American Negro has improved during the past three decades. "There can be no question but that relations between the American Negroes and the balance of the population in the United States have improved during the last generation,"[2] wrote Du Bois. Du Bois offered persuasive evidence to support his opinion: the decline in the number of lynchings, the hiring of Negro policemen in many Southern cities, the increase in the number of Negroes registered to vote, and improvements in education, health care, and housing. The average Negro might not yet be enjoying the same lifestyle as the average white American, but the American Negro is no second-class citizen. His life will continue to improve.

Separation, Not Segregation

Many critics of the race situation in America argue that the Negro is the victim of segregation. Herbert Ravenel Sass, however, has correctly pointed out that "Segregation is sometimes carelessly listed as a synonym of separation, but it is not a true synonym and the difference between the two words is important."[3] It is true that in the United States the white and black races, for the most part, occupy separate social spheres, but the separation of the races is not evidence of the Negro's inferior place in American society.

Most Negroes simply prefer to live near and associate with other Negroes. Negro children prefer to attend a school with other Negro children. In restaurants and motels and on beaches and golf courses, Negroes prefer to be in the company of other Negroes. In that sense, Negroes are no different from other ethnic groups in America. Jews feel comfortable living in neighborhoods with other Jews; hence, certain urban neighborhoods have large concentrations of Jewish people. The same is true for the Irish, Italians, Poles, and other ethnic groups.

The great Negro educator and author Booker T. Washington made this essential point more than a half-century ago in his moving autobiography, *Up from Slavery*. Once while traveling on a train, Washington was invited by some white ladies to join them for dinner in the white passengers' dining car. Washington thought it rude to reject the ladies' kind invitation, but he reported feeling uncomfortable and embarrassed at being the only Negro man eating dinner in a white dining car. He would have felt more comfortable in the company of other Negroes during dinner. Washington eloquently explained the proper relationship between whites and Negroes when he stated, "In all things that are purely social we can be as separate as the fingers, yet one as the hand in all things essential to mutual progress."[4]

Take a walk down Main Street in any bustling Southern city. You will see white women and Negro women walking the avenue with their shopping bags. At the corner gas station, a white mechanic will be repairing an automobile while a Negro man pumps gas. A white police officer might be walking the beat on one street while a colored officer walks his beat a few blocks away. Any separation between the races in America is by custom and preference and is no indication of the Negro's second-class citizenship.

Continued Progress

We must bear in mind that a century ago, most American Negroes were still slaves. Today, slavery is absent from the American landscape, and gone with it are illiteracy, poverty, home-lessness, and other badges of second-class citizenship. During the past fifty years, the situation of America's Negroes has improved significantly. If American Negroes continue to show patience and determination, their position in American society will continue to improve.

1. Quoted in William Dudley, ed., *The Civil Rights Movement: Opposing Viewpoints*. San Diego: Greenhaven Press, 1996, p. 75.

2. Quoted in John Egerton, *Speak Now Against the Day: The Generation Before the Civil Rights Movement in the South*. New York: Alfred A. Knopf, 1995, p. 487.

3. Quoted in Dudley, *The Civil Rights Movement*, p. 76.

4. Booker T. Washington, *Up from Slavery*. New York: Bantam Books, 1970, p. 156.

"Freedom is never voluntarily given by the oppressor; it must be demanded by the oppressed."

American Negroes Should Agitate for Civil Rights

Author's note: This viewpoint is written from an early-1960s perspective.

During the past several years, American Negroes have become more outspoken about their inferior position in American society. In Montgomery and Birmingham, Alabama, in Greensboro, North Carolina, and in other Southern cities, Negroes, sometimes joined by white supporters, have risen up to protest their situation in carefully planned public demonstrations. Many Americans have criticized Negro citizens and their leaders for organizing these mass demonstrations for civil rights. Such demonstrations, however, are morally justified, are absolutely necessary, and are protected by the Constitution of the United States.

Moral Justification

Nearly a decade after the U.S. Supreme Court, in its *Brown v. Board of Education* decision, outlawed segregated public schools and thereby began to erase the color line in American society, the American Negro remains a second-class citizen. Many Negroes still face discrimination when they search for housing and employment. Many schools, workplaces, neighborhoods, and social gathering places remain racially segregated. Many American Negroes still live in poverty.

Negroes have a moral right to protest against these conditions. As James M. Lawson Jr., a member of the Student Nonviolent Coordinating Committee (SNCC) and a leader of the protest demonstrations against segregated eating places in Nashville, Tennessee, stated, "[W]e who are demonstrators are trying to raise what we call the 'moral issue.' That is, we are pointing to the viciousness of racial segregation and prejudice and calling it evil or sin. The matter is not legal, sociological or racial, it is moral and spiritual."[1]

The Negro citizens who boycotted public buses in Montgomery in 1955 to protest that city's bus seating laws; the students who participated in sit-ins at lunch counters in Nashville, Greensboro, and other Southern cities to protest segregated service; and the citizens who marched in Birmingham for civil rights were acting as morally responsible American citizens. They were trying to rid their nation of the moral evils of racial prejudice and discrimination.

Public Demonstrations Are Necessary

In his "Letter from a Birmingham Jail," Reverend Martin

Martin Luther King Jr.

Luther King Jr. stated, "History is the long and tragic story of the fact that privileged groups seldom give up their privileges voluntarily. . . . We know through painful experience that freedom is never voluntarily given by the oppressor; it must be demanded by the oppressed."[2] King is correct when he suggests that American Negroes must demand their civil rights and work aggressively to obtain them, and King is not the only American Negro to put forth that argument. Gordon R. Carey, a field director of the Congress of Racial Equality (CORE), has stated, "It seems to us that the civil rights movement will not get anywhere by merely being patient. We believe that there must be an element of patience, but the Negro community in the South is not willing to wait until next year for the rights which they should have had 10 or 20 years ago."[3]

Negro students have been particularly articulate in emphasizing the necessity of public demonstrations to secure civil rights. An SNCC newsletter made that point during one of the restaurant sit-ins in North Carolina in 1960 two years ago: "We want the world to know that we no longer accept the inferior position of second-class citizenship."[4] A similar sentiment came in a full-page advertisement placed in the *Atlanta Constitution* by a group of college students in Atlanta: "We do not intend to wait placidly for those rights which are already legally and morally ours. . . . Today's youth will not sit by submissively, while being denied all rights, privileges, and joys of life."[5]

Only through public demonstrations can America's Negroes achieve their civil rights. The city council of Montgomery, Alabama, would never have changed its law forcing Negro passengers to sit in the rear seats of buses had the city's Negro citizens not waged a yearlong boycott of the buses. The lunch counters in Nashville and Greensboro began to serve Negro customers only after the initiation of sit-in movements involving hundreds of students. The cities and states of the South will not likely repeal their segregation laws or end their discriminatory customs until Negro citizens demand their civil rights.

A Constitutional Right to Protest

The First Amendment to the U.S. Constitution guarantees "the right of the people peaceably to assemble, and to petition the government for a redress of grievances." By protesting for their civil rights, Negro citizens are exercising their First Amendment rights. The men who crafted the words of the First Amendment understood the need for citizens to articulate their grievances against their government. King is correct in his "Letter from a Birmingham Jail" when he states that today's Negroes who protest for their civil rights are "carrying our whole nation back to those great wells of democracy which were dug deep by the Founding Fathers in the formulation of the Constitution and the Declaration of Independence."[6]

For the most part, the demonstrations organized by King, SNCC, CORE, and other civil rights organizations have been peaceful. The Montgomery bus boycott of the past decade involved Negro citizens simply refusing to ride that city's buses and, instead, walking to work, carpooling, or riding bicycles. No Montgomery bus was damaged; no bus driver was hurt. During the restaurant sit-ins, citizens sat at lunch counters and politely awaited service. The violence that erupted during some of these demonstrations was almost always ignited by angry white citizens or by local police.

In many speeches, King has stressed that all demonstrations for civil rights must be peaceful and nonviolent. In a 1960 speech, King stated, "We will not obey unjust laws or submit to unjust practices. We will do this peacefully, openly, and cheerfully because our aim is to persuade. We adopt the means of nonviolence because our end is a community at peace with itself."[7]

Unjust Laws

Many Americans have expressed concern that these demonstrations for civil rights have sometimes resulted in the breaking of laws. In Birmingham, for example, King was arrested for parading without a permit. Students who participated in the restaurant sit-ins were often arrested for trespassing or disturbing the peace. But as King has argued, there are just laws and unjust laws: "A just law is a man-made code that squares with the moral law or the law of God. An unjust law is a code that is out of harmony with the moral law. . . . Any law that uplifts human personality is just. Any law that degrades human personality is unjust."[8] In advocating the breaking of unjust laws, King is echoing the ideas of Henry David Thoreau, the great American philosopher of the nineteenth century, who argued in his famous essay "Civil Disobedience," "If it [a law] is of such a nature that it requires you to be the agent of injustice to another, then, I say, break the law."[9]

Liberation for the Nation

Today's Negroes who are agitating for their civil rights are not troublemakers determined to create havoc and civil unrest in the United States; they are patriotic Americans determined to secure their civil rights and thereby make the United States a better and more democratic nation. In the words of James Baldwin, the Negro essayist and novelist, this current movement by Negro Americans for civil rights is designed to "force the country to honor its own ideals. . . . The goal of the student movement is nothing less than the liberation of the entire nation from its most crippling attitudes and habits."[10]

1. Quoted in Sanford Wexler, *The Civil Rights Movement: An Eyewitness History*. New York, Facts On File, 1993, p. 127.

2. Martin Luther King Jr., *I Have a Dream: Writings and Speeches That Changed the World*. San Francisco: HarperSanFrancisco, 1992, p. 87.

3. Quoted in Wexler, *The Civil Rights Movement*, p. 129.

4. Quoted in Wexler, *The Civil Rights Movement*, p. 128.

5. Quoted in Wexler, *The Civil Rights Movement*, p. 126.

6. King, *I Have a Dream*, p. 100.

7. King, *I Have a Dream*, p. 69.

8. King, *I Have a Dream*, p. 89.

9. Henry David Thoreau, *Civil Disobedience and Other Essays*. New York: Dover Books, 1993, p. 8.

10. James Baldwin, *Nobody Knows My Name*. New York: Vintage Books, 1961, p. 75.

"Agitation [for civil rights] only worsens relations between the races at precisely the time that racial healing is needed."

American Negroes Should Not Agitate for Civil Rights

Author's note: This viewpoint is written from an early-1960s perspective.

During the past several years, America's Negroes have conducted a series of public demonstrations for the purpose of gaining their civil rights. These demonstrations, however, have succeeded only in escalating tensions between the white and black races in the United States. If American Negroes sincerely believe that they are being denied their rights as U.S. citizens, they should make their appeal for citizenship rights in the courtrooms and legislative houses; they should not create civil unrest in the nation's cities and towns.

Many Negro leaders claim that American Negroes live as second-class citizens. The truth, however, is that much progress has been made in the field of civil rights since the conclusion of World War II. More Negro youths are finishing high school and attending college. The income of the average Negro family has risen dramatically during the past fifteen years, which has allowed Negro families to purchase homes and buy automobiles, televisions, and other consumer products.

Despite this progress, many Negro leaders believe that some

color barriers still exist in American society. If barriers do exist, Negro leaders should make their appeals for their civil rights in courts of law. In the United States, the courts of law are fair and impartial bodies that dictate reasonable solutions for social and legal problems that arise between groups of citizens. During the past several years, the courts have struck down many laws that once restricted the rights of Negro citizens. For example, courts have invalidated laws that segregated public schools, beaches, golf courses, parks, and buses. Another avenue for Negroes with grievances concerning their civil rights is their duly elected legislative bodies. Any group of citizens that believes their citizenship rights are being denied can petition their elected representatives for redress through appropriate legislation. A group of Alabama clergymen, commenting on recent protests over racial problems in the city of Birmingham, offered sound advice for Negroes who believe that their civil rights are being denied: "When rights are consistently denied, a cause should be pressed in the courts and in negotiations among local leaders, and not in the streets."[1]

Civil Unrest

The Negroes' campaign for civil rights often has led to civil unrest, which in the long run is likely to hinder rather than advance the Negroes' efforts to achieve their goal. For example, the restaurant sit-ins of a few years ago—when Negro college students sat at lunch counters in Southern cities and demanded service—often resulted in angry confrontations between whites and Negroes. These sit-ins probably worsened rather than improved relations between the races in the South. Likewise, the so-called freedom rides of the summer of 1961—when groups of boisterous Negroes and white sympathizers rode buses through the South in an attempt to integrate bus terminals—often resulted in violence. A Greyhound bus in Alabama was destroyed by an angry mob of whites. In Montgomery, a confrontation between the freedom riders and angry local citizens erupted in violence. Several freedom riders and a public official were injured. Governor John Patterson of Alabama rightly referred to the freedom riders as "car loads of rabble rousers" traveling from city to city "for the avowed purpose of disobeying our laws, flaunting our customs and traditions and creating racial incidents."[2]

The leaders of these freedom rides claimed that their tactics were intended to be nonviolent. That might be true, but violence often accompanied the freedom rides. Even the *New York Times*, which has generally been sympathetic to the civil rights demonstrations of the past several years, criticized the freedom rides. A *Times* editorial calling for an end to the freedom rides wisely stated, "Non-violence that deliberately provokes violence is a logical contradiction."[3]

Breaking the Law

The most disturbing aspect of the civil rights demonstrations of the past several years has been the willingness of Negro leaders and demonstrators to break the laws intentionally. Demonstrators have routinely broken local ordinances designed to separate the races and, more problematic, often have trespassed on private property and disturbed the peace. Reverend Martin Luther King Jr., who has personally led several of these demonstrations, recently stated, "I submit that an individual who breaks a law that conscience tells him is unjust, and willingly accepts the penalty by staying in jail to arouse the conscience of the community over the injustice, is in reality expressing the very highest respect for law."[4]

If every citizen followed Reverend King's advice—blatantly breaking any law he or she found unworthy—our nation would degenerate into anarchy. If a motorist disagrees with a traffic law, should he simply break that law? How then would we ensure safety on our roadways? What if some citizens find the income tax laws unfair? Do those citizens have a right not to pay their income taxes? For advice on this issue, American citizens should refer to words penned by Abraham Lincoln in 1838:

When I so pressingly urge a strict observance of all the laws, let me not be understood as saying there are no bad laws, nor that grievances may not arise, for the redress of which, no legal provisions have been made. I mean to say no such thing. But I do mean to say, that, although bad laws, if they exist, should be repealed as soon as possible, still while they continue in force, for the sake of example, they should be religiously observed.[5]

A Time for Patience

"The wisest among my race understand that the agitation of questions of social equality is the extremest folly, and that progress in the enjoyment of all the privileges that will come to us must be the result of severe and constant struggle rather than of artificial forcing,"[6] declared the great Negro leader Booker T. Washington in 1895. Washington's words ring true today. Indeed, civil rights and privileges will come to American Negroes if they remain patient and steadfast in their determination to rid America of any remaining racial barriers. To agitate for social justice in the streets of America's towns and cities, however, does not advance the Negroes' cause. Such agitation only worsens relations between the races at precisely the time that racial healing is needed.

1. Quoted in William Dudley, ed., *The Civil Rights Movement: Opposing Viewpoints.* San Diego: Greenhaven Press, 1996, p. 115.

2. Quoted in Sanford Wexler, *The Civil Rights Movement: An Eyewitness History.* New York: Facts On File, 1993, p. 131.

3. Quoted in Taylor Branch, *Parting the Waters: America in the King Years 1954–63.* New York: Simon and Schuster, 1988, p. 478.

4. Martin Luther King Jr., *I Have a Dream: Writings and Speeches That Changed the World.* San Francisco: HarperSanFrancisco, 1992, p. 90.

5. Abraham Lincoln, *Selected Speeches and Writings.* New York: Vintage Books, 1992, p. 18.

6. Booker T. Washington, *Up from Slavery.* New York: Bantam Books, 1970, p. 157.

"Integration cannot be forced peaceably upon the South by a federal court."

The Federal Government Should Not Interfere with State and Local Governments in Civil Rights Matters

Author's note: This viewpoint is written from an early-1964 perspective.

Since the end of the Civil War, the South has dealt with the problem of the Negro. When that bloody conflict ended, 4 million Negro slaves were suddenly free, and the South faced the overwhelming task of feeding, housing, employing, and educating these itinerant people. It was a formidable problem, but with reason and sensitivity, the South was able to integrate the Negro into Southern society. Today, a century after the Civil War, the Southern Negro lives better than Negroes anywhere else on earth. For the most part, Negroes of the South live in decent housing, eat healthy meals, have attained literacy, and earn fair wages as productive members of the South's economy. The South has dealt effectively with the Negro problem.

Nonetheless, now we are hearing an outcry, from a small percentage of disenchanted Negroes in the South and from their supporters in the North, that the federal government must take a more active role in the affairs between the South's white and Negro citizens. This kind of interference from Washington is both ill-timed and counterproductive. The South must be allowed to deal with racial issues in the same reasonable and sensitive way that it has during the past hundred years.

Interference from the Courts

This trend of the federal government interfering in the South's racial matters began ten years ago when the Supreme Court, in the case of *Brown v. Board of Education*, ordered the desegregation of the South's public schools. At the time of that decision, voices of protest arose from the South. For example, Governor Herman Talmadge of Georgia declared, "The people of Georgia believe in, adhere to and will fight for their right under the United States and Georgia constitutions to manage their own affairs."[1] Senator Harry Byrd of Virginia called the Court's decision "the most serious blow that has yet been struck against the rights of states in a matter vitally affecting their authority and welfare."[2] Two years after the *Brown* decision, Southern senators and congressional representatives issued a proclamation calling for its repeal, asserting that the decision "is creating chaos and confusion in the States principally affected. It is destroying the amicable relations between the white and Negro races that have been created through 90 years of patient effort by people of both races."[3]

School systems in the South have been predictably slow in complying with the Supreme Court's order. Today, a decade after that order was issued, only a very small percentage of Negro schoolchildren in the South attend a racially integrated school. Why has compliance with the Court's order taken so long? Because integration cannot be forced peaceably upon the

South by a federal court. Cities and towns in the South should have been allowed to set their own educational policies.

Where integration was forced by court order, relations between the races worsened. In 1957, for example, a federal court ordered the integration of Central High School in Little Rock, Arkansas. The local school board and Governor Orval Faubus of Arkansas understandably opposed this federal interference in the affairs of the state of Arkansas and the city of Little Rock. President Dwight Eisenhower, however, sent federal troops to force Central High to admit nine Negro students. Predictably, tensions arose between Little Rock's white and colored residents, resulting in several days of civil unrest. Moreover, the nine Negro students encountered problems in their classrooms. Their lives were threatened; one colored student was expelled after an argument with white students. Fortunately, no Little Rock residents were seriously hurt or killed, but the crisis at Central High School disrupted the academic year of several hundred high school students.

Forced Integration Results in Civil Unrest

A problem similar to the one in Little Rock occurred at the University of Mississippi in 1962 when James Meredith, a Negro, attempted to enroll. Meredith, after applying in the usual procedure, was turned down by the university, and he protested his rejection in federal court. The court ordered that Meredith be admitted, but when he attempted to register, he faced an angry group of protesters. A near riot occurred at the university and in the town of Oxford. Two people were killed in the violence, and the Mississippi National Guard had to be sent to Oxford to establish order.

Would it not have been wiser to allow the state of Mississippi and the University of Mississippi to work out this problem? Couldn't a committee of state officials, university administrators, faculty members, and students have found some reasonable way to accommodate Mississippi's Negro students? The court's order to admit Meredith naturally led to resentment and frustration among the university's students and the residents of Oxford, which inevitably erupted in violence, costing two innocent people their lives.

Violence and civil unrest also erupted in 1961 when the Interstate Commerce Commission ordered the integration of bus terminals throughout the South. Violence flared last year in the city of Birmingham when Negroes protested in the streets, with the support of President John Kennedy and Attorney General Robert Kennedy. At that time, a group of Alabama clergymen sensibly called for negotiations between local civic leaders to resolve racial problems and for an end to outside interference in Birmingham's racial affairs:

> We agree . . . with certain local Negro leadership which has called for honest and open negotiation of racial issues in our area. And we believe this kind of facing of issues can best be accomplished by citizens of our own metropolitan area, white and Negro, meeting with their knowledge and experience of the local situation.[4]

Civil unrest over racial issues is likely to continue if the federal government tries to force its own solutions on towns and cities across the United States.

The Present Legislation

Presidents John Kennedy and Lyndon Johnson have asked Congress to pass civil rights legislation that will outlaw segregation in privately owned public places, such as restaurants, hotels, movie theaters, and sports arenas. This kind of federal action is exactly the type that will create further tensions between the races throughout the United States. As Senator Richard Russell of Georgia has pointed out, "The use of federal power to force the owner of a dining hall or swimming pool to unwillingly accept those of a different race as guests creates a new and special right for Negroes in derogation of the property rights of all of our people to own and control the fruits of their labor and ingenuity." Senator Russell properly rejects "the idea that federal power may be invoked to compel the mingling of the races in social activities to achieve the nebulous aim of social equality."[5]

Solutions to racial problems forced on states and municipalities by the federal government will not work and will create further civil unrest, leading to a worsening of relations between white and Negro citizens.

1. Quoted in Sanford Wexler, *The Civil Rights Movement: An Eyewitness History*. New York: Facts On File, 1993, p. 47.

2. Quoted in Wexler, *The Civil Rights Movement*, p. 48.

3. Quoted in William Dudley, ed., *The Civil Rights Movement: Opposing Viewpoints*. San Diego: Greenhaven Press, 1996, p. 73.

4. Quoted in Dudley, *The Civil Rights Movement*, p. 114.

5. Quoted in Dudley, *The Civil Rights Movement*, pp. 184, 186.

"The Federal Government has a clear duty to see that Constitutional guarantees of individual liberties . . . are not denied or abridged anywhere in our Union."

The Federal Government Should Take an Active Role in Promoting Civil Rights

Author's note: This viewpoint is written from an early-1964 perspective.

Many people view the civil rights problems that the United States confronts today as a set of local issues that must be dealt with by local and state governments. Although it is true, as former president Harry Truman once suggested, that "There is much that state and local governments can do in providing positive safeguards for civil rights,"[1] the federal government must take the lead in making certain that all Americans, regardless of race, enjoy the benefits and privileges of U.S. citizenship. The courts must enforce civil rights laws already on the books; Congress must propose and pass new civil rights legislation; and the president must ensure that civil rights laws are respected and enforced throughout the United States.

Support from Four Presidents

All four American presidents in the post–World War II era
have embraced the idea that the federal government must play
the lead role in the effort to ensure that all Americans enjoy
their civil rights. Near the end of his first term in office, President Truman, in a special message to Congress, asserted the
need for federal civil rights legislation:

> The Federal Government has a clear duty to see that
> Constitutional guarantees of individual liberties and of
> equal protection under the laws are not denied or
> abridged anywhere in our Union. That duty is shared by
> all three branches of the Government, but it can be fulfilled only if the Congress enacts modern, comprehensive
> civil rights laws, adequate to the needs of the day, and
> demonstrating our continuing faith in the free way of life.[2]

Although Congress never delivered on his request, Truman,
throughout his tenure in office, remained committed to the
idea that the federal government must act decisively on civil
rights issues.

President Dwight Eisenhower did not enter office as an
outspoken advocate of civil rights for Negroes, but he signed
into law the first pieces of federal civil rights legislation since
the Reconstruction Era: the Civil Rights Act of 1957, which
established a civil rights division within the Justice Department and formed a national Commission on Civil Rights, and
the Civil Rights Act of 1960, which attempted to remove restrictions preventing Negro citizens from voting. In September 1957, when Governor Orval Faubus of Arkansas tried to
prevent the integration of Central High School in Little
Rock, Eisenhower sent federal troops to Little Rock to make
sure that the federal court's order to desegregate Central High
would be obeyed.

The late president John Kennedy responded positively to
the outcry for civil rights during his presidency. As Eisen-

hower had done in the Little Rock crisis, Kennedy sent federal troops to the University of Mississippi to ensure that that school obeyed a court order to desegregate by allowing James Meredith, a Negro student, to enroll. Kennedy was also an outspoken supporter of Reverend Martin Luther King Jr.'s campaign to end racial segregation and discrimination in America. In June 1963, five months before his tragic death, Kennedy addressed the American people in a televised speech on the need for new comprehensive civil legislation, declaring that such legislation is necessary because "We face . . . a moral crisis as a country and as a people."[3]

President Lyndon Johnson has vowed to follow through on Kennedy's initiatives in the area of civil rights. On November 27, 1963, less than a week after assuming the presidency, Johnson sent a message to Congress calling for speedy passage of the civil rights bill that Kennedy had sent to Congress the previous June so that "the ideas and ideals which [Kennedy] so nobly represented . . . will be translated into effective action."[4]

The Need for Federal Action

These four American presidents, representing both major political parties, saw the need for action by the federal government in the arena of civil rights because states and municipalities have dragged their feet on these issues. Governors like George Wallace of Alabama, Orval Faubus of Arkansas, and Ross Barnett of Mississippi have, for example, attempted to defy court orders mandating the desegregation of public schools. Southern states have placed legal roadblocks in the path of Negro citizens who have attempted to exercise their constitutional rights to register and vote.

Despite the Supreme Court's 1954 order to desegregate public schools, despite various federal court orders to desegregate beaches, bus terminals, and other public places, the South today remains rigidly segregated. In many areas, Negroes cannot patronize restaurants or hotels; they encounter restricted seating practices in theaters and sports arenas; and they face discrimination when they apply for housing and employment. The Southern states will not end these immoral practices until the federal government forces them to do so through court orders and appropriate legislation.

The Need for Appropriate Legislation

The federal government must act quickly and decisively in the area of civil rights. Specifically, Congress should pass the sweeping civil rights legislation proposed by Presidents Kennedy and Johnson. This bill would end discrimination and segregation in restaurants, hotels, movie theaters, sports arenas, and other privately owned public gathering places. It would also make it illegal for employers to discriminate in their hiring practices.

In addition, Congress should enact legislation that prevents discrimination in housing. This kind of discrimination is practiced widely, in both the North and South. Finally, Congress should pass a voting rights act that removes all barriers preventing American citizens of any race and any region from exercising their right to vote. This right is fundamental and should not be denied to any American citizen who is eligible to vote.

A National Problem

Reverend Martin Luther King Jr. has stated that the racial issue "that we confront in America is not a sectional but a national problem. Injustice anywhere is a threat to justice everywhere."[5] President John Kennedy echoed King when he stated that civil rights "is not a sectional issue. Difficulties over segregation and discrimination exist in every city, in every state of the Union, producing in many cities a rising tide of discontent that threatens the public safety."[6]

National problems require the attention of the federal government. All three branches of the federal government must work aggressively to ensure that the civil rights of all Americans are protected and that all American citizens, regardless of race, enjoy the privileges and opportunities that derive from American citizenship.

1. Quoted in Sanford Wexler, *The Civil Rights Movement: An Eyewitness History.* New York: Facts On File, 1993, p. 27.

2. Quoted in William Dudley, ed., *The Civil Rights Movement: Opposing Viewpoints.* San Diego: Greenhaven Press, 1996, p. 57.

3. Quoted in Dudley, *The Civil Rights Movement*, p. 180.

4. Quoted in Wexler, *The Civil Rights Movement*, p. 196.

5. Martin Luther King Jr., *I Have a Dream: Writings and Speeches That Changed the World.* San Francisco: HarperSanFrancisco, 1992, p. 67.

6. Quoted in Dudley, *The Civil Rights Movement*, p. 179.

CHAPTER 2

Goals and Strategies of the Civil Rights Movement

"To create one nation has proved to be a hideously difficult task; there is certainly no need now to create two, one black and one white."

Integration Should Be the Primary Goal of the Civil Rights Movement

Author's note: This viewpoint is written from a mid-1960s perspective.

For more than a decade, black citizens across the United States have been agitating for their civil rights. In Montgomery, Alabama, in 1955, black residents protested discriminatory seating practices on municipal buses. In 1960, black college students sat in at restaurants to protest discriminatory serving practices. During the summer of 1961, freedom riders rode buses throughout the South to force the integration of public bus terminals. In 1963, the black citizens of Birmingham, Alabama, took to the streets to protest discriminatory hiring policies in downtown stores and shops. That summer, more than 250,000 white and black Americans gathered in Washington, D.C., in a massive protest for jobs and freedom. In 1965, thousands of black and white citizens marched from Selma to Montgomery, Alabama, to demand that the state's black citizens be allowed to register to vote and cast their ballots unimpeded on election day.

Martin Luther King Jr. (left of center behind truck) joins more than 250,000 protesters in a civil rights march through the streets of Washington, D.C. in August 1963.

The common denominator in these stirring public protests, the common call made by black citizens and their white allies, is a demand for full integration into all aspects of American life. The primary goal of this movement for civil rights has been, and should continue to be, an end to racial segregation and discrimination, resulting in a peacefully integrated American society.

Segregation Makes Black Americans Second-Class Citizens

A decade ago, the U.S. Supreme Court, in the landmark case *Brown v. Board of Education*, ruled that segregated schools cause irreparable damage to black schoolchildren. Black children who attend a segregated school and grow up in a segregated society begin to see themselves as inferior citizens, unfit for full participation in American life. In his moving "Letter from a Birmingham Jail," Reverend Martin Luther King Jr. recorded the pain experienced by black parents who must raise their children in a segregated society: "You suddenly find your tongue twisted and your speech stammering as you seek to explain to your six-year-old daughter why she can't go to the public amusement park that has just been advertised on television, and see tears welling up in her little eyes when she is told that Funtown is closed to colored children, and see depressing clouds of inferiority begin to form in her little mental sky."[1]

As that child grows into adulthood, she learns that she cannot be hired in certain places of employment, that she cannot dine in certain restaurants, and that she cannot live in certain sections of town. She begins to believe what her segregated society is telling her: that she is a second-class citizen. Moreover, as James Farmer, founder of the Congress of Racial Equality, has noted, "The damage [of segregation] to Negroes is [not just] psychological; it is also economic. Negroes occupy the bottom of the economic ladder, the poorest jobs, the lowest paying jobs. Last to be hired, and first to be fired, so that today the percentage of unemployed Negroes is twice as high as that of whites."[2]

Segregation Damages All of American Society

Farmer has pointed out that segregation damages whites as well. He recalls how many whites in his home state of Texas intimidated and insulted black people. "I wondered what was happening to these people," he says, "how their minds were being twisted, as mine and others like me had had our minds twisted by this double-edged sword of prejudice." Farmer rightly calls segregation "an American disease."[3] This disease makes blacks inferior citizens and turns too many whites into hateful racists.

King has articulately argued that the United States cannot fulfill its ambitious national goals unless it rids itself of the evils of segregation and discrimination: "It is a trite yet urgently true observation that if America is to remain a first-class nation, it cannot have second-class citizens."[4] The Declaration of Independence boldly asserts the proposition "that all men are created equal." The U.S. Constitution guarantees all citizens "equal protection of the laws." As the late president John Kennedy stated, "This Nation was founded by men of many nations and backgrounds. It was founded on the principle that all men are created equal, and that the rights of every man are diminished when the rights of one man are threatened."[5] The time has come for America's democracy to reach full maturity by ending racial segregation and discrimination. "Now is the time to make real the promises of democracy," said King in his "I Have a Dream" speech. "Now is the time to rise from the dark and desolate valley of segregation to the sunlit path of racial justice."[6]

Black Segregationists

In the past few years, some black leaders, notably those affiliated with the Black Muslim sect of the Nation of Islam, have called for a sharp division in American society along racial lines. Elijah Muhammad, Malcolm X, and other Black Muslim leaders have argued that black citizens will never be treated fairly in an integrated society, that they will always be in an inferior position socially, politically, and economically. These leaders argue that black Americans should be given two or three states as their own to rule as they see fit. Presumably, all black Americans would move to these few states, and no whites would live there.

This solution to America's racial problems is grossly impractical. As James Farmer has argued, in response to Malcolm X's call for a separate black society within the United States, "You must tell us, Mr. X, if you seriously think that the Senate of the United States which has refused or failed for all these years to pass a strong Civil Rights Bill, you must tell us if you really think that this Senate is going to give us, to give you, a black state."[7] Would all blacks want to leave their homes and jobs and migrate to a black state? Would the white people living in that state willingly leave without protest?

The Black Muslim argument for a separate black state also ignores history. Blacks came to these shores even before the pilgrims; they, too, are Americans. They fought in the American Revolution, the Civil War, both world wars of this century, and the Korean War—and they are serving in Vietnam today. Their history and their destiny are interwoven with America's history and destiny. They share communities, workplaces, and churches with white Americans. Reverend Milton Galamison, a pastor from Brooklyn, New York, made this very point in a debate with Malcolm X in 1963:

> When then we speak of integration or separation as alternatives, we must consider the degree to which the Negro is already woven into the pattern of American life. We have been integrated at the level of sowing. It is in the area of reaping that we have been short changed. . . . We have planted the tree. Shall we not demand the fruit?[8]

A Fairly Integrated Society

In his long essay titled *The Fire Next Time*, James Baldwin, the author from Harlem, rejects the separatist rhetoric of Elijah Muhammad and argues instead for a peacefully integrated American society:

> In short, we, the black and white, deeply need each other here if we are really to become a nation—if we are really, that is, to achieve our identity, our maturity, as men and women. To create one nation has proved to be a hideously difficult task; there is certainly no need now to create two, one black and one white.[9]

Baldwin is correct. The solution for America's troubling racial problems is not further segregation. It is integration—a fairly integrated society in which black and white citizens live in harmony, a society in which all citizens receive equal protection of the law and equal treatment socially, politically, and economically.

1. Martin Luther King Jr., *I Have a Dream: Writings and Speeches That Changed the World*. San Francisco: HarperSanFrancisco, 1992, p. 88.

2. Quoted in William Dudley, ed., *The Civil Rights Movement: Opposing Viewpoints*. San Diego: Greenhaven Press, 1996, p. 92.

3. Quoted in Dudley, *The Civil Rights Movement*, p. 92.

4. King, *I Have a Dream*, p. 67.

5. Quoted in Dudley, *The Civil Rights Movement*, p. 178.

6. King, *I Have a Dream*, p. 103.

7. Quoted in Dudley, *The Civil Rights Movement*, p. 98.

8. Quoted in Dudley, *The Civil Rights Movement*, p. 91.

9. James Baldwin, *The Fire Next Time*. New York: Vintage Books, 1962, p. 97.

"Integration will not solve the problems of black America."

Integration Should Not Be the Primary Goal of the Civil Rights Movement

Author's note: This viewpoint is written from a mid-1960s perspective.

Integration has been the rallying cry of many black Americans involved in the civil rights protests of the past decade. The aim of these black citizens is lofty: the complete dismantling of the barriers in American society that restrict nonwhite people and reduce them to second-class citizens. These black integrationists reason that if black people are able to integrate American society—mix with whites in schools, communities, workplaces, and social gathering places—they will receive fair and equal treatment in all aspects of American life. The leader of the integrationists is Reverend Martin Luther King Jr., who, in his often-quoted speech delivered during the March on Washington for Jobs and Freedom of August 1963, dreamed of a future time in America when "all of God's children—black men and white men, Jews and Gentiles, Catholics and Protestants—will be able to join hands and sing in the words of the old Negro spiritual, 'Free at last, free at last; thank God Almighty, we are free at last.'"[1]

Reverend King and his fellow integrationists are honorable but misguided—honorable because they wish to improve the lot of black citizens by striking down segregation laws and practices that demean blacks, but misguided in their belief that integration is the primary means by which black citizens will achieve freedom and equality. Integration will not solve the problems of black America.

Blacks Receive Unequal Treatment in an Integrated Society

Much of American society has been integrated for more than two hundred years. The Southern antebellum plantations were integrated. Today, Atlanta and Birmingham, Detroit and New York City, San Francisco and Los Angeles are integrated cities; both whites and blacks live in these places. Many public schools in America are integrated. Workplaces are integrated; General Motors and Sears and Roebuck employ both white and black workers. The U.S. armed forces have been integrated since 1948.

So, has integration been good for black people? Has it placed them on equal footing with whites in American society? No, it has not. In integrated societies, the black person is always in second place. On the integrated antebellum plantation, the black slave picked the cotton in the hot sun, while the white master sat on the shaded veranda counting his profits. In integrated Birmingham today, the white man manages the store for $10 per hour, while the black man mops the floor for $1 per hour. In integrated New York City, the white family lives in a posh Westside penthouse, while the black family lives in the Harlem slums. The white army officer sits in an office in Washington, while the black soldier sits in the mud in Vietnam. In integrated societies, the black person is always in an inferior position.

Nation of Islam leader Malcolm X is correct when he points out that very few blacks profit from integration. Only middle- and upper-class black people, not the black masses, actually live well in an integrated American society:

We who are black in the black belt, or black community, or black neighborhood, can easily see that our
people who settle for integration are usually the middle-
class so-called Negroes, who are in the minority. Why?
Because they have confidence in the white man; they
have absolute confidence that you will change. They
believe that they can change you, they believe that
there is still hope in the American dream.[2]

Integration will improve the lives of few of the 20 million
black people who live in the United States.

The White Man Is Not an Ally

Malcolm X has been criticized for referring to the white
American as "a common enemy . . . a common oppressor, a
common exploiter, and a common discriminator."[3] Many
whites are oppressors and exploiters; many more are indifferent to the plight of black America; and very few whites can be
relied on as allies in black people's struggle for human dignity.
White Americans have had more than three hundred years to
right the injustices perpetrated upon blacks. It took the white
man more than 250 years to rid America of slavery. For the
next hundred years, white society imposed upon black society
a system of Jim Crow laws that kept black people second-class
citizens. In the South, whites restricted black people to the
plantations; in the North, blacks were channeled into the urban ghettoes.

   Now black people are being told that if they integrate white
society—if they go to school with whites and share workplaces, neighborhoods, churches, restaurants, beaches, and
movie theaters—they will become the equals of whites. Is such
a change likely to occur overnight? Malcolm X is correct
when he expresses skepticism about white America's ability to
recognize blacks as equal citizens:

   [W]e don't think that it is possible for the American
   white man in sincerity to take the action necessary to

correct the unjust conditions that twenty million black people here are made to suffer morning, noon, and night. And because we don't have any hope or confidence or faith in the American white man's ability to bring about a change in the injustices that exist, instead of asking or seeking to integrate into the American society we want to face the facts of the problem the way they are, and separate ourselves.[4]

A Separate Black Society

Elijah Muhammad, Malcolm X, and other black leaders involved in the movement to separate blacks from white American society have proposed the establishment of separate states or regions of the United States where black people would live and govern themselves. Such an effort would be highly desirable. Blacks would establish their own schools, their own businesses, their own communities. Black entrepreneurs would own property and provide decent housing with reasonable rent payments. Rather than growing up in an integrated society that reminds them of their inferiority every day, black children would grow up as proud members of communities run by black people. Blacks would not have to face job discrimination, police brutality, and the many other social problems that they face in an integrated society. They would vote for their own political leaders on election day, and black voters would not be turned away at the ballot box or forced to choose between two white candidates, both of whom are indifferent to the plight of black people.

But establishing a separate black society within the United States would be difficult. Would white America willingly surrender even two or three states where black people could live? Would a black state merely become a colony of white America, ripe for exploitation? Even if a separate black state within the United States is not feasible at this time, black Americans can still effectively separate themselves from white society. They can, for example, establish and patronize their own businesses, gain control of school boards in black communities, pool their resources to buy and upgrade the crumbling housing projects in black communities now owned by white slumlords, and establish centers to exhibit black artistic projects.

All black American citizens should begin to realize that they will not soon achieve their rights and dignities in a society dominated by whites. Well-meaning black leaders who are calling for integration are naïve and misguided. As stated in the charter of the Organization of Afro-American Unity,

Careful evaluation of recent experiences shows that "integration" actually describes the process by which a white society is (remains) set in a position to use, whenever it chooses to use and however it chooses to use, the best talents of non-white people. This power-web continues to build a society wherein the best contributions of Afro-Americans, in fact of all non-white people, would continue to be absorbed without note or exploited to benefit a fortunate few while the masses of both white and non-white would remain unequal and unbenefited.[5]

1. Martin Luther King Jr., *I Have a Dream: Writings and Speeches That Changed the World.* San Francisco: HarperSanFrancisco, 1992, pp. 105–106.

2. Quoted in William Dudley, ed., *The Civil Rights Movement: Opposing Viewpoints.* San Diego: Greenhaven Press, 1996, p. 104.

3. Quoted in Clayborne Carson et al., eds., *The Eyes on the Prize Civil Rights Reader.* New York: Penguin Books, 1991, p. 249.

4. Quoted in Dudley, *The Civil Rights Movement*, p. 104.

5. Quoted in Abraham Chapman, ed., *New Black Voices: An Anthology of Contemporary Afro-American Literature.* New York: Mentor Books, 1972, p. 570.

"Violence, even in self-defense, creates more problems than it solves."

Black Americans Should Use Nonviolent Means to Secure Their Civil Rights

Author's note: This viewpoint is written from a mid-1960s perspective.

Black Americans' struggle to gain their civil rights during the past decade has been bitter and difficult. Black protesters and their white comrades have gained many victories in this struggle: Segregation laws have been struck down; racist practices have been eliminated; and key pieces of civil rights legislation have been enacted by federal, state, and local governments. But these victories have been costly. Civil rights protesters, both black and white, have lost their lives in the struggle. Hundreds of demonstrators have been beaten by the police and by angry white resisters; hundreds have spent nights in uncomfortable jail cells.

Some black leaders, frustrated by this slow and difficult progress, have become angry. Now they are saying that courtroom petitions take too long and that peaceful demonstrations are ineffective. These leaders are calling on black people to arm themselves and prepare for a more aggressive civil rights struggle; they are claiming that violent means might be necessary to achieve their honorable goals. Although they may be impatient with the sluggish progress of the civil rights struggle, black Americans should shut their ears to those who advocate the use of violence in the effort to gain civil rights.

A Movement Founded on Nonviolent Principles

The civil rights movement that began in the United States ten years ago was built on a solid foundation of principles of nonviolence. Reverend Martin Luther King Jr., Reverend Ralph Abernathy, and other leaders of this movement strongly stressed the use of nonviolent tactics to achieve their goals. In one of his first public addresses, at the commencement of the Montgomery bus boycott of 1955–1956, King stressed the need for a nonviolent protest. "We are impatient for justice," said King, "but we will protest with love. There will be no violence on our part."[1] A decade later, King's commitment to nonviolent tactics remains strong. He recently wrote in *Ebony* magazine that "violence, even in self-defense, creates more problems than it solves. Only a refusal to hate or kill can put an end to the chain of violence in the world and lead us toward a community where men can live together without fear."[2]

King's lieutenants in the civil rights struggle—Abernathy, James Farmer, and Bayard Rustin—have remained committed to the use of nonviolent strategies to achieve their goals. The Student Nonviolent Coordinating Committee (SNCC), which spearheaded the restaurant sit-ins and freedom rides of 1960–1961, has always stressed nonviolent tactics. Before major civil rights demonstrations, SNCC and other civil rights organizations have sponsored workshops to train protesters in the use of nonviolent methods of resistance.

Nonviolence Works

Nonviolent strategies work. To protest the bus-seating laws of Montgomery, Alabama, King advocated a bus boycott. For more than a year, that city's black residents refused to patronize the municipal buses. The protesters made their point: A federal court struck down Montgomery's discriminatory bus-seating laws.

In the winter and spring of 1960, college students throughout the South staged sit-ins in restaurants that would not serve black customers. Protesters sat patiently as police and local white residents abused them verbally and physically. Within several weeks, however, lunch counters in Greensboro, North Carolina; Nashville, Tennessee; and other Southern cities began to cease their discriminatory serving policies and wait on black customers. Those nonviolent protests also worked.

In the spring of 1963, King and his Southern Christian Leadership Conference (SCLC) led a series of nonviolent demonstrations in the city of Birmingham, Alabama, which King called "probably the most thoroughly segregated city in the United States."[3] The entire nation watched as Bull Connor, the Birmingham chief of police, set loose on unarmed protesters attack dogs and policemen armed with billy clubs and high-pressure water hoses. The demonstrators were, for the most part, nonviolent; the police, however, tried to turn a peaceful protest into a full-scale race riot. The piety of the nonviolent protesters moved citizens across the United States and, more important, stirred federal officials in Washington into action. After a month of demonstrations, the city of Birmingham commenced negotiations with SCLC to dismantle racial barriers in that city. Those demonstrations also worked.

A month later, in June 1963, President John Kennedy, moved by the dignity and courage of the nonviolent protesters in Birmingham and elsewhere, addressed the nation in a televised speech on the need for federal legislation to end racial discrimination in employment and in restaurants, hotels, theaters, and other public gathering places. In his speech, Kennedy paid special tribute to black citizens who were demonstrating for civil rights: "They are acting not out of a sense of legal duty but out of a sense of human decency."[4] Kennedy's life ended before his proposed legislation received approval by Congress. But on July 2, 1964, President Lyndon Johnson signed into law the landmark Civil Rights Act of 1964, which accomplished the goals that Kennedy had set. Thus, the nonviolent demonstrations in Birmingham and elsewhere led directly to the passage of the single most important piece of civil rights legislation of the twentieth century.

A Better America

From the start, King has stated that his goal in prompting black citizens to agitate for their civil rights is to make America a better country, a place where all citizens are treated equally. King has never wanted to make white America his enemy; he envisions white and black Americans living together in a new age of harmony, which cannot happen if black civil rights protesters engage in violent and destructive behavior. King made this point in his very first national address in 1957:

> There is the danger that those of us who have lived so long under the yoke of oppression, those of us who have been exploited and trampled over, those of us who have had to stand amid the tragic midnight of injustice and indignities will enter the new age with hate and bitterness. But if we retaliate with hate and bitterness, the new age will be nothing but a duplication of the old age. We must blot out the hate and injustice of the old age with the love and justice of the new. This is why I believe so firmly in nonviolence. Violence never solves problems. It only creates new and more complicated ones.[5]

James Baldwin, the Harlem essayist, made this same point in his poignant essay *The Fire Next Time*: "I . . . must oppose any attempt that Negroes may make to do to others what has been done to them. I think I know—we see it around us every day—the spiritual wasteland to which that road leads. It is so simple a fact and one that is so hard, apparently, to grasp: *Whoever debases others is debasing himself.*" [6]

1. Quoted in Harvard Sitkoff, *The Struggle for Black Equality 1954–1980.* New York: Hill and Wang, 1981, p. 50.

2. Martin Luther King Jr., *I Have a Dream: Writings and Speeches That Changed the World.* San Francisco: HarperSanFrancisco, 1992, p. 130.

3. King, *I Have a Dream,* p. 85.

4. Quoted in William Dudley, ed., *The Civil Rights Movement: Opposing Viewpoints.* San Diego: Greenhaven Press, 1996, p. 182.

5. King, *I Have a Dream,* p. 21.

6. James Baldwin, *The Fire Next Time.* New York: Vintage Books, 1962, p. 83.

"The stone wall which blocks expectant Negroes in every town and village of the hard-core South . . . will have to be crumbled by hammer blows."

Nonviolent Actions Might Not Be Sufficient for Black Americans to Secure Their Civil Rights

Author's note: This viewpoint is written from a mid-1960s perspective.

Reverend Martin Luther King Jr. and other leaders of the civil rights movement of the past ten years have stressed the use of nonviolent tactics—the boycott, the sit-in, and the peaceful protest march—to achieve their goals. To some extent, this nonviolent approach has been successful; King has razed some of the barriers in the Deep South that restrict and demean blacks. Overall, however, progress in the area of civil rights has come slowly. Much of the South remains segregated, and the Northern black citizen still suffers from poverty, inadequate education, job and housing discrimination, police brutality, and other indignities of second-class citizenship. Furthermore, during the past few years, we have seen a violent backlash from angry whites against those involved in this civil rights movement: Churches and homes have been bombed; black civil rights advocates and their white comrades have been beaten and killed; and government officials in some parts of the South have imposed even more restrictions on the lives of black citizens.

Nonviolent tactics might be effective in some cases and in some areas of the South. In some circumstances and in some areas, however, more aggressive tactics might be necessary to secure black citizens their rights and to protect blacks from a violent backlash from angry whites.

Meeting Nonviolence with Violence

Since its beginnings in Montgomery, Alabama, a decade ago, the civil rights crusade has been fundamentally a nonviolent effort, but angry white citizens and their elected and appointed officials have used violent tactics to obstruct it. During the restaurant sit-in movement of 1960, policemen and angry whites perpetrated acts of violence on peaceful protesters. The freedom riders of 1961—civil rights workers who rode buses into Southern cities to desegregate bus terminals—were often greeted by angry mobs of violent whites; in one case, a bus was destroyed. In September 1962, the Ku Klux Klan destroyed by dynamite four black churches in Georgia. A year later, a black church in Birmingham, Alabama, was bombed during a Sunday school program, killing four young black girls, an action that King properly called "one of the most vicious, heinous crimes ever perpetrated against humanity."[1] King's own home has been firebombed by racists eager to stop his movement.

Medgar Evers

The body count of slain civil rights workers is increasing. In June 1963, Medgar Evers, a field secretary for the National Association for the Advancement of Colored People, was killed by gunshots outside of his home in Jackson, Mississippi.

No one has been convicted of this crime. A year later, the bodies of three civil rights workers, two whites and one black, were found near Philadelphia, Mississippi. That crime, too, remains unpunished.

Can nonviolent tactics prevent these kinds of crimes? Can a peaceful protest march change the heart of a white racist who is angry and hateful enough to bomb a church during a Sunday school program? Could a few verses of the hymn "We Shall Overcome" convince a gunman aiming at a civil rights worker to lower his rifle? Clearly, tactics more aggressive than sit-ins, protest marches, and boycotts might be necessary when black civil rights protesters confront the perpetrators of these kinds of crimes.

The Right to Self-Defense

The charter of the Organization of Afro-American Unity correctly points out that "the Constitution of the U.S.A. clearly affirms the right of every American citizen to bear arms."[2] Indeed, the Second Amendment to the Constitution guarantees that "the right of the people to keep and bear arms shall not be infringed." The men who framed that article were concerned that a powerful and despotic federal government might impose its will upon the citizens; hence, the citizens might need to arm themselves to meet that threat. The framers of the Second Amendment seem to have had in mind the situation that many black protesters face in the South today. When the government, in the form of the local police, attacks citizens with billy clubs, tear gas, high-pressure water hoses, and attack dogs, don't those citizens, under the Second Amendment, have the right to arm themselves for defense?

In an article in the journal *Liberation* several years ago, Robert F. Williams, a former chapter leader of the National Association for the Advancement of Colored People, cited two cases in which white men indicted for abusing black women in the South were acquitted of their crimes by all-white juries. One of the men had entered the home of a pregnant black woman and attempted to rape her. Sickened by the absence of justice in these cases, Williams concluded, "I believe Negroes must be willing to defend themselves, their women, their children and their homes. They must be willing to die and to kill their assailants."[3] Similarly, Nation of Islam leader Malcolm X has stated, "If it must take violence to get the black man his human rights in this country, I'm *for* violence exactly as you know the Irish, the Poles, or Jews would be if they were flagrantly discriminated against."[4]

Would it have been morally wrong for the black woman cited in Williams's article to have kept a gun in her house and to have used it on the white intruder who attempted to rape her? Would it have been wrong for a group of black citizens in Georgia to bomb the home of that state's head Klansman after the Klan dynamited four black churches?

Nonviolence Will Not Work Everywhere

Nonviolence tactics will not work in all circumstances and all places. Howard Zinn, a former professor of history at Spelman College in Atlanta, points to the so-called Albany Movement of 1961–1962 as an example of a case where nonviolent tactics failed. King's nonviolent protest campaign in Albany, Georgia, failed to achieve its goal of desegregating that city. Zinn concedes that in some Southern cities—such as Richmond, Memphis, Nashville, and Atlanta—nonviolent protests have accounted for "the first cracks" in a formerly solid segregated social structure. But Zinn goes on to state, "I am now convinced that the stone wall which blocks expectant Negroes in every town and village of the hard-core South, a wall stained with the blood of children, as well as others, and with an infinite capacity to absorb the blood of more victims—will have to be crumbled by hammer blows."[5]

In the mid-1770s the American colonists, rejecting the oppressive policies of their mother country, armed themselves for battle. In 1861, the Southern states, rejecting the policies of the federal government of the United States, armed themselves for battle. Today, black Americans might have to do the same. As Robert F. Williams stated, "It is instilled at an early age that men who violently and swiftly rise to oppose tyranny are virtuous. . . . Nowhere in the annals of history does the record show a people delivered from bondage by patience alone."[6]

1. Martin Luther King Jr., *I Have a Dream: Writings and Speeches That Changed the World*. San Francisco: HarperSanFrancisco, 1992, p. 116.

2. Quoted in Abraham Chapman, ed., *New Black Voices: An Anthology of Contemporary Afro-American Literature*. New York: Mentor Books, 1972, p. 559.

3. Quoted in William Dudley, ed., *The Civil Rights Movement: Opposing Viewpoints*. San Diego: Greenhaven Press, 1996, p. 160.

4. Malcolm X and Alex Haley, *The Autobiography of Malcolm X*. New York: Ballantine Books, 1964, p. 422.

5. Quoted in Dudley, *The Civil Rights Movement*, pp. 156–57.

6. Quoted in Dudley, *The Civil Rights Movement*, p. 160.

CHAPTER 3

Historical Assessment of the Civil Rights Movement

"The civil rights movement 'began the transformation of America into a more open and just society.'"

The Civil Rights Movement Was a Success

On the night before he died, Reverend Martin Luther King Jr. delivered one of his most eloquent speeches. He concluded his stirring address by asserting that he was not concerned about living a long life because God had allowed him to "go up the mountain" and view the promised land: "And I've seen the promised land. I may not get there with you. But I want you to know tonight, that we, as a people, will get to the promised land." For King the promised land was an America in which all citizens, regardless of race, would be treated fairly and equally, a nation in which, in King's words, people "will not be judged by the color of their skin but by the content of their character."[1]

At the turn of the twenty-first century, the United States is not yet the promised land that King envisioned. Racial strife and racial inequalities, particularly in the area of economics, continue to plague the nation. But the civil rights movement that King championed brought the United States far down the road toward that promised land. As the late Ronald Brown, secretary of commerce during part of the presidency of Bill Clinton, stated, the civil rights movement "began the transformation of America into a more open and just society."[2]

An End to Legalized Segregation

Americans born after 1970 might find it difficult to believe that racial segregation was, before 1954, not only widely practiced but also implemented, in the South at least, by the force of law. In 1896, in the case of *Plessy v. Ferguson*, the U.S. Supreme Court had ruled that states and municipalities could pass laws that separate the races in public places. Thus, most Southern states passed laws that segregated public schools, parks, restaurants, hotels, even restrooms and water fountains. The Court's decision in the 1954 case *Brown v. Board of Education* ended legal segregation in public schools and prompted lower courts to strike down other segregation statutes. Moreover, as historian David Halberstam has noted, "The *Brown v. Board* decision not only legally ended segregation, it deprived segregationist practices of their moral legitimacy as well."[3]

The *Brown* case was advanced by Thurgood Marshall and other attorneys employed by the National Association for the Advancement of Colored People. Encouraged by their success in *Brown*, these lawyers mounted a legal challenge to the segregationist laws of the South that ultimately ended legalized segregation in the United States.

Landmark Legislation

The civil rights movement accounted for two of the most important pieces of federal legislation in the twentieth century—the Civil Rights Act of 1964 and the Voting Rights Act of 1965. After the *Brown* decision, courts began to strike down laws that segregated *publicly owned* social gathering places, such as bus depots, public beaches, and parks. But the owner of a *privately owned* hotel or restaurant could still refuse to serve black patrons. Civil rights demonstrators throughout the South—those who sat in in restaurants in Greensboro, North Carolina, and those who marched in Birmingham, Alabama—alerted American citizens to the fundamental injustice of laws that segregated these social gathering places.

Moved by the courage of civil rights demonstrators, President John Kennedy sent to Congress legislation that became known as the Civil Rights Act of 1964, which outlawed segregationist practices in privately owned public facilities.

The Voting Rights Act, passed after the Selma-to-Montgomery march of 1965, fundamentally changed American politics. Congressman Charles Rangel of New York has asserted that "No legislative act growing out of the civil rights movement has done more to promote the cause of political equality for black Americans than the passage of the Voting Rights Act of 1965."[4] That law resulted in the registration of millions of black voters throughout the South. In 1965, there were about 250 black elected officials in the United States, the overwhelming majority in the North; in 2000, there are almost 9,000. Black mayors have been elected in Baltimore, Atlanta, Chicago, Los Angeles, and other major cities. At the turn of the twenty-first century, African Americans form a voting bloc that no politician can ignore.

Educational and Economic Gains

As a result of gains made during the civil rights movement, a college education is attainable for today's African American students. In 1950, approximately 113,000 African Americans attended college; in 2000, that number increased tenfold to 1.1 million students. To a great extent that was made possible because courageous men like James Meredith demanded that Southern colleges and universities open their doors to qualified black students. Today's high school senior completing a college application might find it hard to believe that Governor George Wallace of Alabama once stood guard at the gates of his state's university to prevent black students from registering. No governor can legally do what Wallace did in 1963; if a governor tried such a move today, that governor would be quickly chased from office. In addition, most colleges now offer courses in African American history and literature—an outgrowth of the black studies movement that accompanied the civil rights movement.

In 1963 Alabama governor George Wallace personally blocked the entrance of the University of Alabama and refused to allow black students to register for classes.

African Americans still lag behind white Americans in economic accomplishments. The black unemployment rate is higher than the national average. The per capita income for black families drags behind the average income for white families. Nonetheless, mainly because of gains realized during the civil rights movement, an increasing percentage of African Americans have moved from poverty to the middle class. Companies that have implemented affirmative action policies have given qualified African American job applicants special considerations in hiring and promotion.

Advances for Other Minorities

Joseph Rauh Jr., an attorney active in the civil rights struggle, accurately pointed out that the civil rights movement did not help only African Americans: "It also resulted in a legal revolution for women, for Hispanics, for other minorities, for the disabled and for the aged. What you had was a total shift in the legal system of America to protect those who cannot protect themselves."[5]

During the last quarter of the twentieth century, federal, state, and local governments enacted legislation to help women and other minorities gain equal footing in employment and other endeavors. In 1990, President George Bush signed into law the Americans with Disabilities Act, banning discrimination against those with physical or mental handicaps in employment, public accommodations, and transportation. Today, schools, post offices, libraries, even restaurants and businesses have ramps so that people restricted to wheelchairs have access. This legislation, an outgrowth of the civil rights movement, reflects a sea change in the mind-set of the American public, a realization that minorities have the same rights as other Americans as they go to work and school and engage in social activities.

The United States is far from perfect in its record of making sure that all Americans enjoy their civil rights, but it is a more just nation than it was in 1950, before Thurgood Marshall, Martin Luther King Jr., and others began their crusade for civil rights. As Hodding Carter, a white Mississippian who served as press secretary in the administration of President Jimmy Carter, asserted, the civil rights movement "did not produce utopia, but it brought us all out of a moral and political hell."[6]

1. Martin Luther King Jr., *I Have a Dream: Writings and Speeches That Changed the World*. San Francisco: HarperSanFrancisco, 1992, pp. 203, 104.

2. Quoted in Sanford Wexler, *The Civil Rights Movement: An Eyewitness History*. New York: Facts On File, 1993, p. 265.

3. David Halberstam, *The Fifties*. New York: Villard Books, 1993, p. 423.

4. Quoted in Wexler, *The Civil Rights Movement*, p. 264.

5. Quoted in Wexler, *The Civil Rights Movement*, p. 263.

6. Quoted in Wexler, *The Civil Rights Movement*, p. 264.

"Martin Luther King's dream of an American society free of segregation and discrimination, a society with equal opportunity for all, remains unfulfilled."

The Civil Rights Movement Was a Failure

The civil rights movement of the 1950s and '60s resulted in some improvement in the lives of African Americans. Segregation sanctioned by law was outlawed, as were overt segregationist practices that prevented black people from eating in certain restaurants, staying in certain hotels, and sitting in the front seats of public buses. Federal legislation passed during the 1960s outlawed many of the barriers that prevented black citizens in the South from voting. Under pressure, Southern colleges and universities opened their gates to African American students.

But the United States remains, in many ways, a house divided by race. As Senator Bill Bradley once remarked, "Slavery was our original sin, just as race remains our unresolved dilemma."[1] The main goals of the civil rights movement were to destroy the barriers that separated white and black Americans and to eliminate racial discrimination so that African Americans would no longer be treated as second-class citizens. Despite some important accomplishments, the civil rights movement failed to achieve those noble goals.

An Abrupt Conclusion

The civil rights movement began to lose its momentum after 1965. The movement's loss of energy is evidenced by the frustration among black citizens that led to the urban race riots of 1965, 1967, and 1968. Despite the end of legalized segregation, despite the passage of the Civil Rights Act of 1964 and the Voting Rights Act of 1965, many black Americans were frustrated by the slow progress in the area of civil rights. This frustration erupted into major race riots in Watts, California, in 1965; in Newark, New Jersey, and Detroit in 1967; and in Washington, D.C., and other cities in 1968 in response to the assassination of Reverend Martin Luther King Jr. The causes of such riots were many—police brutality, the oppressive poverty that was a part of urban African American life, the inadequacy of government services in African American ghettoes—but the riots certainly revealed that many black Americans still felt like second-class citizens. The civil rights movement had not improved the lives of the vast African American underclass who lived in urban America.

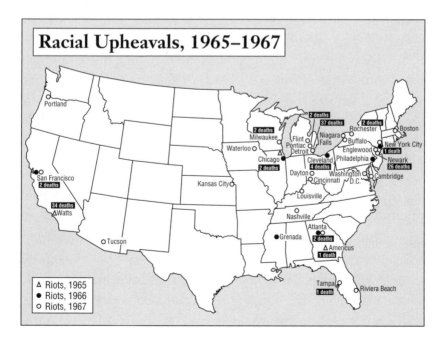

Racial Upheavals, 1965–1967

- △ Riots, 1965
- ● Riots, 1966
- ○ Riots, 1967

The civil rights movement ended when a white racist murdered Martin Luther King Jr. Had King lived, he might have been able to build on his impressive accomplishments during his thirteen years of public life. No charismatic civil rights leaders emerged after King's death, and King's movement lost its energy. The Rodney King riot in Los Angeles in 1992 provides evidence that King's dream for an America unburdened by the dilemma of race remains unfulfilled. African American residents in Los Angeles rioted for three days after four white police officers were acquitted of using excessive force against Rodney King, an African American motorist detained by police, though a videotape clearly showed the white officers brutally beating King. The riot resulted in fifty-one deaths and $1 billion in property damage. Those who rioted undoubtedly saw the Rodney King beating and the acquittal of the officers who beat him as evidence that black citizens had yet to achieve equal protection under the law.

Segregation Persists in America

Although Martin Luther King Jr. boldly asserted, in 1957, that "Old Man Segregation is on his deathbed,"[2] the United States remains, in many ways, a segregated society at the turn of the twenty-first century. Take public schools, for example. Historians of the civil rights movement point to the U.S. Supreme Court decision in the case of *Brown v. Board of Education* as the event that brought about the end of legally sanctioned racial segregation in the United States. But in 2000, millions of African American children attend urban schools that no white children attend. The white children attend suburban schools in all-white neighborhoods, and these schools are generally better equipped and better funded than urban schools that enroll nonwhite students.

In 1989, Jonathan Kozol, one of the foremost critics of American education, studied several schools and found that school boards with essentially white student populations outspent schools whose populations were virtually all nonwhite by a two-to-one margin. "What seems unmistakable, but, oddly enough, is rarely said in public settings nowadays," states Kozol, "is that the nation, for all practice and intent, has turned its back upon the moral implications, if not the ramifications, of the *Brown* decision."[3]

Legislation enacted during the civil rights movement may have outlawed racial segregation and discrimination, but both still exist in American society. For example, a 1999 study by the U.S. Department of Housing and Urban Development documented persistent racial discrimination in housing. A 1989 study conducted by *Harvard Business Review* revealed widespread consumer discrimination against African Americans. Studies of law enforcement tactics revealed that African Americans are more likely than whites to be stopped by police and frisked for drugs or weapons and more likely to be stopped on the roadways for traffic violations.

Economic Disparities

Economically, African Americans still lag behind white Americans. The unemployment rate for African Americans has remained approximately 50 percent higher than the unemployment rate for white Americans. An alarmingly high percentage of African Americans still live below the government-defined poverty line. The average yearly income for African American families is only about two-thirds of the average income for whites. Even African Americans who have moved into the middle class are not as financially well off as middle-class whites. A 1999 study revealed that the typical white family that earns $40,000 per year has a net worth of around $80,000, while the black family with the same income has a net worth of only about $40,000.

These economic disparities are unlikely to disappear in the near future. Young people who are educationally prepared for a fast-changing technological society will qualify for high-paying jobs, while those lacking in skills will qualify only for low-paying jobs in the service economy. Too many African American young people complete their education without the skills needed to compete in a technology-based economy; these individuals will lag behind their peers economically for their entire lives. In his famous "I Have a Dream" speech, Martin Luther King Jr. lamented that the black American "lives on a lonely island of poverty in the midst of a vast ocean of material prosperity."[4] That is still the case today.

A Dream Deferred

Harvard Sitkoff concludes his book on the civil rights movement, *The Struggle for Black Equality 1954–1980*, with a chapter titled "The Dream Deferred." Indeed, Martin Luther King Jr.'s dream of an American society free of segregation and discrimination, a society with equal opportunity for all, remains unfulfilled. According to Sitkoff, the United States remains "a deeply divided and unequal society":

> The black struggle had brought significant changes. It achieved substantial progress. . . . Yet the full promise of the civil-rights revolution was unrealized. Prejudice, discrimination, and segregation, both subtle and blatant, continued to poison social relations. Neither the franchise nor the demolition of legal racism had resulted in equality or justice.[5]

The goals of the civil rights movement were ambitious; its leaders were courageous individuals who devoted their lives to a noble cause. But their effort fell short.

1. Quoted in Sanford Wexler, *The Civil Rights Movement: An Eyewitness History*. New York: Facts On File, 1993, p. 265.

2. Martin Luther King Jr., *I Have a Dream: Writings and Speeches That Changed the World*. San Francisco: HarperSanFrancisco, 1992, p. 24.

3. Jonathan Kozol, *Savage Inequalities: Children in America's Schools*. New York: Harper-Perennial, 1991, p. 4.

4. King, *I Have a Dream*, p. 102.

5. Harvard Sitkoff, *The Struggle for Black Equality 1954–1980*. New York: Hill and Wang, 1981, p. 228.

STUDY QUESTIONS

Chapter 1

1. Why did Americans begin to fervently debate the issue of civil rights after the U.S. victory over Nazi Germany in World War II?

2. Viewpoints 1 and 2 offer specific evidence to support their views on whether American Negroes are second-class citizens. Identify the evidence provided by each side in this debate. In your view, which side has presented more persuasive evidence?

3. Viewpoint 3 argues that breaking a law is sometimes necessary in civil rights protests, whereas Viewpoint 4 argues that disrespect for the law will lead to social anarchy. Are there circumstances under which breaking a law is morally justified? If so, what kinds of laws can be broken? Must the breaking of a law be done in public? Must the law be broken in a nonviolent manner?

4. Do those who oppose the use of federal authority in civil rights issues (see Viewpoint 5) seem sincere in their desire to solve civil rights issues locally, or are the opponents of federal interference merely looking for an excuse to defend the status quo and keep black citizens in an inferior position in Southern society? Should the federal government be concerned with how a state or municipality runs its schools and its local businesses? Since public schools are paid for mainly through local property taxes, should the local government—rather than the federal government—establish educational policies?

5. Does the federal government, through legislation, have the right to order the owners of restaurants, hotels, and similar facilities to serve all customers, regardless of race? Or do the owners of a restaurant or hotel have the right to serve whomever they please?

Chapter 2

1. Can black Americans be treated fairly if they live in communities where the majority of the population is white? Or would black Americans be better off living in separate black communities, where blacks own the businesses, run the schools, and establish policies, as suggested in Viewpoint 2?

2. Does racial integration foster racial tolerance and an understanding between people of different races? Are people who attend racially integrated schools or work in racially integrated

workplaces more likely to form positive relationships with individuals of another race than people in segregated schools or workplaces?

3. Do you believe that people have the right to use violent tactics to obtain their civil rights, as suggested in Viewpoint 4? Under what circumstances might violence be justifiable?

4. Do you think the Jews of Europe during the 1930s could have used nonviolent tactics to resist Adolf Hitler's Final Solution, his effort to exterminate all European Jews? Would the tactics used in the United States during the civil rights movement (see Viewpoint 3)—the boycott, the protest march, the sit-in—have been successful in Nazi Germany? Why or why not?

5. What other tactics—besides the boycott, protest march, and sit-in—can be employed by citizens who wish to bring about social change by using nonviolent means?

Chapter 3

1. Should the civil rights movement still be considered a success even if all of its primary goals were not attained to the fullest degree?

2. Both Viewpoints 1 and 2 offer evidence to support their claims concerning the success of the civil rights movement. Which viewpoint offers the more persuasive evidence? Explain.

3. Viewpoint 1 suggests that some companies give qualified African American employees priority in hiring and promotion. Do you think this is fair, or is it discrimination against white employees?

4. If today's African American political, business, and religious leaders gathered at a conference to begin a second civil rights movement, what should be the goals of this new movement? What should be its highest priorities?

APPENDIX OF DOCUMENTS

Document 1: The Fourteenth and Fifteenth Amendments to the Constitution

In the wake of the Civil War, Congress proposed two constitutional amendments that attempted to deliver the rights of citizenship to newly freed slaves. The Fourteenth Amendment, ratified in 1868, guaranteed all U.S. citizens "equal protection of the laws." The Fifteenth Amendment made it illegal to prohibit a citizen from voting "on account of race, color, or previous condition of servitude."

The Fourteenth Amendment
Ratified July 9, 1868

Section 1. All persons born or naturalized in the United States and subject to the jurisdiction thereof, are citizens of the United States and of the State wherein they reside. No State shall make or enforce any law which shall abridge the privileges or immunities of citizens of the United States; nor shall any State deprive any person of life, liberty, or property, without due process of law; nor deny to any person within its jurisdiction the equal protection of the laws.

The Fifteenth Amendment
Ratified February 3, 1870

Section 1. The right of citizens of the United States to vote shall not be denied or abridged by the United States or by any State on account of race, color, or previous condition of servitude.

Section 2. The Congress shall have power to enforce this article by appropriate legislation.

The U.S. Constitution.

Document 2: The *Plessy v. Ferguson* Decision

In 1896, the United States heard a case involving Homer Plessy, a black man who had been arrested and fined in Louisiana for traveling in a whites-only train car. The Court ruled against Plessy, asserting that the Fourteenth Amendment was not designed "to abolish distinctions based upon color." This decision established the "separate but equal" doctrine, allowing legislatures to pass laws to segregate the races in schools, parks, restaurants, and other gathering places. An excerpt of the decision, written by Justice Henry Billings Brown, appears below.

The object of the [Fourteenth] amendment was undoubtedly to enforce the absolute equality of the two races before the law, but in the nature of things it could not have been intended to abolish distinctions based upon color, or to enforce social, as distinguished from political equality, or a commingling of the two races upon terms unsatisfactory to either. Laws permitting, and even requiring, their separation in places where they are liable to be brought into contact do not necessarily imply the inferiority of either race to the other, and have been generally, if not universally, recognized as within the competency of the state legislatures in the exercise of their police power. The most common instance of this is connected with the establishment of separate schools for white and colored children, which has been held to be a valid exercise of the legislative power even by courts of States where the political rights of the colored race have been longest and most earnestly enforced. . . .

So far, then, as a conflict with the Fourteenth Amendment is concerned, the case reduces itself to the question whether the statute of Louisiana is a reasonable regulation, and with respect to this there must necessarily be a large discretion on the part of the legislature. In determining the question of reasonableness it is at liberty to act with reference to the established usages, customs and traditions of the people, and with a view to the promotion of their comfort, and the preservation of the public peace and good order. Gauged by this standard, we cannot say that a law which authorizes or even requires the separation of the two races in public conveyances is unreasonable, or more obnoxious to the Fourteenth Amendment than the acts of Congress requiring separate schools for colored children in the District of Columbia, the constitutionality of which does not seem to have been questioned, or the corresponding acts of state legislatures.

We consider the underlying fallacy of the plaintiff's argument to consist in the assumption that the enforced separation of the two races stamps the colored race with a badge of inferiority. If this be so, it is not by reason of anything found in the act, but solely because the colored race chooses to put that construction upon it. . . .

Legislation is powerless to eradicate racial instincts or to abolish distinctions based upon physical differences, and the attempt to do so can only result in accentuating the difficulties of the present situation. If the civil and political rights of both races be equal one cannot be inferior to the other civilly or politically. If one race be inferior to the other socially, the Constitution of the United States cannot put them upon the same plane.

Plessy v. Ferguson, 163 U.S. 537.

Document 3: Justice Harlan's Dissent in *Plessy v. Ferguson*

The Supreme Court's vote in the case of Plessy v. Ferguson *went 7–1 against Homer Plessy. The sole justice who took Plessy's side was John Harlan, who argued that the Fourteenth Amendment prevented legislative bodies from considering the race of citizens "when the civil rights of those citizens are involved." According to Harlan, the U.S. Constitution recognizes no ruling class of citizens: "In respect of civil rights, all citizens are equal before the law."*

I deny that any legislative body or judicial tribunal may have regard to the race of citizens when the civil rights of those citizens are involved. Indeed, such legislation, as that here in question, is inconsistent not only with that equality of rights which pertains to citizenship, National and State, but with the personal liberty enjoyed by every one within the United States. . . .

The white race deems itself to be the dominant race in this country. And so it is, in prestige, in achievements, in education, in wealth and in power. So, I doubt not, it will continue to be for all time, if it remains true to its great heritage and holds fast to the principles of constitutional liberty. But in view of the Constitution, in the eye of the law, there is in this country no superior, dominant, ruling class of citizens. There is no caste here. Our Constitution is color-blind, and neither knows nor tolerates classes among citizens. In respect of civil rights, all citizens are equal before the law. The humblest is the peer of the most powerful. The law regards man as man, and takes no account of his surroundings or of his color when his civil rights as guaranteed by the supreme law of the land are involved. It is, therefore, to be regretted that this high tribunal, the final expositor of the fundamental law of the land, has reached the conclusion that it is competent for a State to regulate the enjoyment by citizens of their civil rights solely upon the basis of race. . . .

The arbitrary separation of citizens, on the basis of race, while they are on a public highway, is a badge of servitude wholly inconsistent with the civil freedom and the equality before the law established by the Constitution. It cannot be justified upon any legal grounds.

If evils will result from the commingling of the two races upon public highways established for the benefit of all, they will be infinitely less than those that will surely come from state legislation regulating the enjoyment of civil rights upon the basis of race. We boast of the freedom enjoyed by our people above all other peoples. But it is difficult to reconcile that boast with a state of the law which, practically, puts the brand of servitude and degradation upon a large class of our fellow-citizens, our equals before the law. The thin disguise of "equal" accommodations for passengers in railroad coaches will not mislead any one, nor atone for the wrong this day done.

Plessy v. Ferguson, 163 U.S. 537.

Document 4: The Supreme Court's Decision in *Brown v. Board of Education of Topeka, Kansas*

Between 1949 and 1951, the National Association for the Advancement of Colored People filed lawsuits against several segregated public school systems, asserting that black students who attended segregated schools received an inferior education and, hence, were deprived of their Fourteenth Amendment right to "equal protection of the laws." These school segregation cases, combined under the general title of Brown v. Board of Education of Topeka, Kansas, *found their way to the U.S. Supreme Court in 1953. On May 17, 1954, the Court ruled unanimously that segregated public schools deprived black students of equal protection of the law by providing them with an inferior education. The decision, part of which is excerpted here, was written by Chief Justice Earl Warren.*

In approaching this problem, we cannot turn the clock back to 1868 when the [Fourteenth] Amendment was adopted, or even to 1896 when *Plessy v. Ferguson* was written. We must consider public education in the light of its full development and its present place in American life throughout the Nation. Only in this way can it be determined if segregation in public schools deprives these plaintiffs of the equal protection of the laws.

Today, education is perhaps the most important function of state and local governments. Compulsory school attendance laws and the great expenditures for education both demonstrate our recognition of the importance of education to our democratic society. It is required in the performance of our most basic public responsibilities, even service in the armed forces. It is the very foundation of good citizenship. Today it is a principal instrument in awakening the child to cultural values, in preparing him for later professional training, and in helping him to adjust normally to his environment. In these days, it is doubtful that any child may reasonably be expected to succeed in life if he is denied the opportunity of an education. Such an opportunity, where the state has undertaken to provide it, is a right which must be made available to all on equal terms.

We come then to the question presented: Does segregation of children in public schools solely on the basis of race, even though the physical facilities and other "tangible" factors may be equal, deprive the children of the minority group of equal educational opportunities? We believe that it does. . . .

Such considerations apply with added force to children in grade and high schools. To separate them from others of similar age and qualifications solely because of their race generates a feeling of inferiority as to their status in the community that may affect their hearts and minds in a way unlikely ever to be undone. The effect of this separation on their educational opportunities was well stated by a finding in the Kansas case by a court which nevertheless felt compelled to rule against the Negro plaintiffs:

> Segregation of white and colored children in public schools has a detrimental effect upon the colored children. The impact is greater when it has the sanction of the law; for the policy of separating the races is usually interpreted as denoting the inferiority of the negro group. A sense of inferiority affects the motivation of the child to learn. Segregation with the sanction of law, therefore, has a tendency to [retard] the educational and mental development of Negro children and to deprive them of some of the benefits they would receive in a racial[ly] integrated school system.

Whatever may have been the extent of psychological knowledge at the time of *Plessy v. Ferguson*, this finding is amply supported by modern authority. Any language in *Plessy* v. *Ferguson* contrary to this finding is rejected.

We conclude that in the field of public education the doctrine of "separate but equal" has no place. Separate educational facilities are inherently unequal. Therefore, we hold that the plaintiffs and others similarly situated for whom the action have been brought are, by reason of the segregation complained of, deprived of the equal protection of the laws guaranteed by the Fourteenth Amendment. This disposition makes unnecessary any discussion whether such segregation also violates the Due Process Clause of the Fourteenth Amendment.

Brown v. Board of Education of Topeka, Kansas, 347 U.S. 483.

Document 5: The Montgomery Bus Boycott

On December 1, 1955, Rosa Parks, secretary of the Montgomery, Alabama, chapter of the National Association for the Advancement of Colored People, was arrested for refusing to surrender her bus seat to a white passenger, as required by municipal law. Montgomery's black citizens united behind Reverend Martin Luther King Jr. in a yearlong bus boycott. The citizens' published resolution, which originally appeared in the Birmingham World, *a black newspaper, is excerpted here. The boycott ended on December 21, 1956, after the city of Montgomery complied with a U.S. Supreme Court order to desegregate Montgomery's municipal buses.*

WHEREAS, there are thousands of Negroes in the city and county of Montgomery who ride busses owned and operated by the Montgomery City Lines, Incorporated, and

WHEREAS, said citizens have been riding busses owned and operated by said company over a number of years, and on many occasions have been insulted, embarrassed and have been made to suffer great fear of bodily harm by drivers of busses owned and operated by said bus company, and

WHEREAS, the drivers of said busses have never requested a white passenger riding on any of its busses to relinquish his seat and stand so that a Negro may take his seat; however, said drivers have on many occasions too numerous to mention requested Negro passengers on said busses to relinquish their seats and stand so that white passengers may take their seats, and

WHEREAS, said citizens of Montgomery city and county pay their fares just as all other persons who are passengers on said busses, and are entitled to fair and equal treatment, and

WHEREAS, there has been any number of arrests of Negroes caused by drivers of said busses and they are constantly put in jail for refusing to give white passengers their seats and stand. . . .

WHEREAS, said citizens of Montgomery city and county believe that they have been grossly mistreated as passengers on the busses owned and operated by said bus company in spite of the fact that they are in the majority with reference to the number of passengers riding on said busses.

Be It Resolved As Follows:

1. That the citizens of Montgomery are requesting that every citizen in Montgomery, regardless of race, color or creed, to refrain from riding busses owned and operated in the city of Montgomery by the Montgomery City Lines, Incorporated until some arrangement has been worked out between said company and the Montgomery City Lines, Incorporated.

2. That every person owning or who has access to automobiles use their automobiles in assisting other persons to get to work without charge.

3. That the employers of persons whose employees live a . . . distance from them, as much as possible afford transportation to your own employees.

4. That the Negro citizens of Montgomery are ready and willing to send a delegation of citizens to the Montgomery City Lines to discuss their grievances and to work out a solution for the same.

Be it further resolved that we have not, are not, and have no intentions of using an unlawful means or any intimidation to persuade persons not to ride the Montgomery City Lines' busses. However, we call upon your consciences, both moral and spiritual, to give your whole-hearted support to this undertaking. We believe we have [a just] complaint and we are willing to discuss this matter with the proper officials.

Birmingham World, December 13, 1955.

Document 6: The Southern Manifesto

In March 1956, one hundred senators and congressmen from the South signed a declaration opposing the Supreme Court's decision in the Brown v. Board of Education *case. The document, later called the "Southern Manifesto," was signed by powerful politicians such as Senator Sam Ervin, Senator William Fulbright, and Senator Strom Thurmond. The document suggests the strong opposition that the school desegregation plan would meet throughout the South.*

The unwarranted decision of the Supreme Court in the public school cases is now bearing the fruit always produced when men substitute naked power for established law.

The Founding Fathers gave us a Constitution of checks and balances because they realized the inescapable lesson of history that no man or group of men can be safely entrusted with unlimited power. They framed this Constitution with its provisions for change by amendment in order to secure the fundamentals of government against the dangers of temporary popular passion or the personal predilections of public office-holders.

We regard the decision of the Supreme Court in the school cases as a clear abuse of judicial power. It climaxes a trend in the Federal Judiciary undertaking to legislate, in derogation of the authority of Congress, and to encroach upon the reserved rights of the States and the people.

The original Constitution does not mention education. Neither does the 14th amendment nor any other amendment. The debates preceding the submission of the 14th amendment clearly show that there was no intent that it should affect the system of education maintained by the States.

The very Congress which proposed the amendment subsequently provided for segregated schools in the District of Columbia.

When the amendment was adopted in 1868, there were 37 States of the Union. Every one of the 26 States that had any substantial racial differences among its people, either approved the operation of segregated schools already in existence or subsequently established such schools by action of the same lawmaking body which considered the 14th amendment.

As admitted by the Supreme Court in the public school case (*Brown v. Board of Education*), the doctrine of separate but equal schools "apparently originated in *Roberts v. City of Boston* (1849), upholding school segregation against attack as being violative of a State constitutional guarantee of equality." This constitutional doctrine began in the North, not in the South, and it was followed not only in Massachusetts, but in Connecticut, New York, Illinois, Indiana, Michigan, Minnesota, New Jersey, Ohio, Pennsylvania and other northern States until they, exercising their rights as States through the constitutional processes of local self-government, changed their school systems.

In the case of *Plessy v. Ferguson* in 1896 the Supreme Court expressly declared that under the 14th amendment no person was denied any of his rights if the States provided separate but equal public facilities. This decision has been followed in many other cases. It is notable that the Supreme Court, speaking through Chief Justice [William H. Taft] a former President of the United States, unanimously declared in 1927 in *Lum v. Rice* that the "separate but equal" principle is "within the discretion of the State in regulating its public schools and does not conflict with the 14th amendment."

This interpretation, restated time and again, became a part of the life of the people of many of the States and confirmed their habits, customs, traditions, and way of life. It is founded on elemental humanity and common sense, for parents should not be deprived by Government of the right to direct the lives and education of their own children.

Though there has been no constitutional amendment or act of Congress changing this established legal principle almost a century old, the Supreme Court of the United States, with no legal basis for such action, undertook to exercise their naked judicial power and substituted their personal political and social ideas for the established law of the land.

This unwarranted exercise of power by the Court, contrary to the Constitution, is creating chaos and confusion in the States principally affected. It is destroying the amicable relations between the white and Negro races that have been created through 90 years of patient effort by the good people of both races. It has planted hatred and suspicion where there has been heretofore friendship and understanding.

Without regard to the consent of the governed, outside agitators are threatening immediate and revolutionary changes in our public-school systems. If done, this is certain to destroy the system of public education in some of the States.

With the gravest concern for the explosive and dangerous condition created by this decision and inflamed by outside meddlers:

We reaffirm our reliance on the Constitution as the fundamental law of the land.

We decry the Supreme Court's encroachments on rights reserved to the States and to the people, contrary to established law, and to the Constitution.

We commend the motives of those States which have declared the intention to resist forced integration by any lawful means.

We appeal to the States and people who are not directly affected by these decisions to consider the constitutional principles involved against the time when they too, on issues vital to them, may be the victims of judicial encroachment.

Even though we constitute a minority in the present Congress, we have full faith that a majority of the American people believe in the dual system of government which has enabled us to achieve our greatness and will in time demand that the reserved rights of the States and of the people be made secure against judicial usurpation.

We pledge ourselves to use all lawful means to bring about a reversal of this decision which is contrary to the Constitution and to prevent the use of force in its implementation.

In this trying period, as we all seek to right this wrong, we appeal to our people not to be provoked by the agitators and trouble-makers invading our States and to scrupulously refrain from disorder and lawless acts.

Congressional Record, 84th Congress, 2nd session (March 12, 1956).

Document 7: The Student Nonviolent Coordinating Committee (SNCC) Statement of Purpose

On the weekend of April 15, 1960, a group of college students involved with the civil rights movement met at Shaw University in Raleigh, North Carolina, to discuss strategy. That group formed SNCC (pronounced "snick"), which cosponsored the freedom rides (to desegregate Southern bus terminals) and other civil rights protests. At the end of the weekend conference, the Reverend James Lawson was selected to draft SNCC's statement of purpose, which was adopted on May 14, 1960.

We affirm the philosophical or religious ideal of nonviolence as the foundation of our purpose, the pre-supposition of our faith, and the manner of our action. Nonviolence as it grows from Judaic-Christian traditions seeks a social order of justice permeated by love. Integration of human endeavor represents the crucial first step towards such a society.

Through nonviolence, courage displaces fear; love transforms hate. Acceptance dissipates prejudice; hope ends despair. Peace dominates war; faith reconciles doubt. Mutual regard cancels enmity. Justice for all overthrows injustice. The redemptive community supersedes systems of gross social immorality.

Love is the central motif of nonviolence. Love is the force by which God binds man to himself and man to man. Such love goes to the extreme; it remains loving and forgiving even in the midst of hostility. It matches the capacity of evil to inflict suffering with an even more enduring capacity to absorb evil, all the while persisting in love.

By appealing to conscience and standing on the moral nature of human existence, nonviolence nurtures the atmosphere in which reconciliation and justice become actual possibilities.

James Lawson, "Student Nonviolent Coordinating Committee Statement of Purpose," May 14, 1960.

Document 8: The Argument for a Separate Black State

Some black civil rights leaders criticized Martin Luther King's call for a fully integrated American society, arguing, instead, for a separate black state within the United States. Malcolm X, a spokesman for the Black Muslim sect of the Nation of Islam, put forth this position in a debate at Cornell University with James Farmer of the Congress of Racial Equality on March 7, 1962. Their comments were later printed in the journal Dialogue. *The following is an excerpt from Malcolm X's speech during that debate.*

The good point in all of this is that there is an awakening going on among whites in America today, and this awakening is manifested in this way: two years ago you didn't know that there were black people in this country who didn't want to integrate with you; two years ago the white public had been brainwashed into thinking that every black man in this country wanted to force his way into your community, force his way into your schools, or force his way into your factories; two years ago you thought that all you would have to do is give us a little token integration and the race problem would be solved. Why? Because the people in the black community who didn't want integration were never given a voice, were never given a platform, were never given an opportunity to shout out the fact that integration would never solve the problem. And it has only been during the past year that the white public has begun to realize that the problem will never be solved unless a solution is devised acceptable to the black masses, as well as the black bourgeoisie—the upper-class or middle-class Negro. And when the whites began to realize that these integration-minded Negroes were in the minority, rather than in the majority, then they began to offer an open forum and give those who want separation an opportunity to speak their mind too.

We who are black in the black belt, or black community, or black neigh-borhood, can easily see that our people who settle for integration are usu-ally the middle-class so-called Negroes, who are in the minority. Why? Because they have confidence in the white man; they have absolute confi-dence that you will change. They believe that they can change you, they believe that there is still hope in the American dream. But what to them is an American dream to us is an American nightmare, and we don't think that it is possible for the American white man in sincerity to take the ac-tion necessary to correct the unjust conditions that twenty million black people here are made to suffer morning, noon, and night. And because we don't have any hope or confidence or faith in the American white man's ability to bring about a change in the injustices that exist, instead of asking or seeking to integrate into the American society we want to face the facts of the problem the way they are, and separate ourselves. And in separating ourselves this doesn't mean that we are anti-white, or anti-American, or anti-anything. We feel that if integration all these years hasn't solved the problem yet, then we want to try something new, something different, and something that is in accord with the conditions as they actually exist.

"Separation or Integration? A Debate at Cornell University," *Dialogue*, May 1962.

Document 9: President Kennedy Addresses the Nation on the Need for Civil Rights Legislation

On June 11, 1963, President John Kennedy, reacting to the many civil rights demonstrations that took place during his first two years in office, addressed the American people on the need for new civil rights legislation. Specifically, Kennedy asked Congress to pass a law making discrimination illegal in hotels, restaurants, theaters, retail stores, and other similar establishments. He also praised the efforts of civil rights activists who had worked to improve their communities. The legislation that Kennedy called for was debated in Congress for more than a year. In July 1964, several months after Kennedy's death, Congress passed the landmark Civil Rights Act of 1964, which President Lyndon Johnson signed into law on July 2.

Good evening, my fellow citizens.

This afternoon, following a series of threats and defiant statements, the presence of Alabama National Guardsmen was required on the University of Alabama to carry out the final and unequivocal order of the United States District Court of the Northern District of Alabama. That order called for the admission of two clearly qualified young Alabama residents who happened to have been born Negro.

That they were admitted peacefully on the campus is due in good mea-sure to the conduct of the students of the University of Alabama, who met their responsibilities in a constructive way.

I hope that every American, regardless of where he lives, will stop and examine his conscience about this and other related incidents. This Nation was founded by men of many nations and backgrounds. It was founded on the principle that all men are created equal, and that the rights of every man are diminished when the rights of one man are threatened.

Today we are committed to a worldwide struggle to promote and protect the rights of all who wish to be free. And when Americans are sent to Viet-Nam or West Berlin, we do not ask for whites only. It ought to be possible, therefore, for American students of any color to attend any public institution they select without having to be backed up by troops.

It ought to be possible for American consumers of any color to receive equal service in places of public accommodation, such as hotels and restaurants and theaters and retail stores, without being forced to resort to demonstrations in the street, and it ought to be possible for American citizens of any color to register and to vote in a free election without interference or fear of reprisal.

It ought to be possible, in short, for every American to enjoy the privileges of being American without regard to his race or his color. In short, every American ought to have the right to be treated as he would wish to be treated, as one would wish his children to be treated. But this is not the case. . . .

We are confronted primarily with a moral issue. It is as old as the scriptures and is as clear as the American Constitution.

The heart of the question is whether all Americans are to be afforded equal rights and equal opportunities, whether we are going to treat our fellow Americans as we want to be treated. If an American, because his skin is dark, cannot eat lunch in a restaurant open to the public, if he cannot send his children to the best public school available, if he cannot vote for the public officials who represent him, if, in short, he cannot enjoy the full and free life which all of us want, then who among us would be content to have the color of his skin changed and stand in his place? Who among us would then be content with the counsels of patience and delay?

One hundred years of delay have passed since President Lincoln freed the slaves, yet their heirs, their grandsons, are not fully free. They are not yet freed from the bonds of injustice. They are not yet freed from social and economic oppression. And this Nation, for all its hopes and all its boasts, will not be fully free until all its citizens are free. . . .

Next week I shall ask the Congress of the United States to act, to make a commitment it has not fully made in this century to the proposition that race has no place in American life or law. The Federal judiciary has upheld that proposition in a series of forthright cases. The executive branch has adopted that proposition in the conduct of its affairs, including the employment of Federal personnel, the use of Federal facilities, and the sale of federally financed housing.

But there are other necessary measures which only the Congress can provide, and they must be provided at this session. The old code of equity law under which we live commands for every wrong a remedy, but in too many communities, in too many parts of the country, wrongs are inflicted on Negro citizens and there are no remedies at law. Unless the Congress acts, their only remedy is in the street.

I am, therefore, asking the Congress to enact legislation giving all Americans the right to be served in facilities which are open to the public—hotels, restaurants, theaters, retail stores, and similar establishments.

This seems to me to be an elementary right. Its denial is an arbitrary indignity that no American in 1963 should have to endure, but many do.

I have recently met with scores of business leaders urging them to take voluntary action to end this discrimination and I have been encouraged by their response, and in the last two weeks over 75 cities have seen progress made in desegregating these kinds of facilities. But many are unwilling to act alone, and for this reason, nationwide legislation is needed if we are to move this problem from the streets to the courts.

I am also asking Congress to authorize the Federal Government to participate more fully in lawsuits designed to end segregation in public education. We have succeeded in persuading many districts to desegregate voluntarily. Dozens have admitted Negroes without violence. Today a Negro is attending a State-supported institution in every one of our 50 States, but the pace is very slow.

Too many Negro children entering segregated grade schools at the time of the Supreme Court's decision 9 years ago will enter segregated high schools this fall, having suffered a loss which can never be restored. The lack of an adequate education denies the Negro a chance to get a decent job.

The orderly implementation of the Supreme Court decision, therefore, cannot be left solely to those who may not have the economic resources to carry the legal action or who may be subject to harassment.

Other features will be also requested, including greater protection for the right to vote. But legislation, I repeat, cannot solve this problem alone. It must be solved in the homes of every American in every community across our country.

John F. Kennedy, *The Public Papers of the Presidents of the United States: John F. Kennedy, 1961–1963*. Washington, DC: U.S. Government Printing Office, 1962–1964.

Document 10: Reverend Martin Luther King Jr.'s Dream for a New America

On August 28, 1963, several civil rights organizations sponsored a March on Washington for Jobs and Freedom. About 250,000 civil rights protesters gathered at the Lincoln Memorial for a rally that included speeches from prominent civil rights leaders. The keynote speaker was the Reverend Martin Luther King Jr., who delivered his famous "I Have a Dream" speech, which concluded with his dream for an America free from the burdens of race.

So I say to you, my friends, that even though we must face the difficulties of today and tomorrow, I still have a dream. It is a dream deeply rooted in the American dream that one day this nation will rise up and live out the true meaning of its creed—we hold these truths to be self-evident, that all men are created equal.

I have a dream that one day on the red hills of Georgia, sons of former slaves and sons of former slave-owners will be able to sit down together at the table of brotherhood.

I have a dream that one day, even the state of Mississippi, a state sweltering with the heat of injustice, sweltering with the heat of oppression, will be transformed into an oasis of freedom and justice.

I have a dream my four little children will one day live in a nation where they will not be judged by the color of their skins but by the content of their character. I have a dream today!

I have a dream that one day, down in Alabama, with its vicious racists, with its governor having his lips dripping with the words of interposition and nullification, that one day, right there in Alabama, little black boys and black girls will be able to join hands with little white boys and white girls as sisters and brothers. I have a dream today!

I have a dream that one day every valley shall be exalted, every hill and mountain shall be made low, the rough places shall be made plain, and the crooked places shall be made straight and the glory of the Lord will be revealed and all flesh shall see it together.

This is our hope. This is the faith that I go back to the South with.

With this faith we will be able to hew out of the mountain of despair a stone of hope. With this faith we will be able to transform the jangling discords of our nation into a beautiful symphony of brotherhood.

With this faith we will be able to work together, to pray together, to struggle together, to go to jail together, to stand up for freedom together, knowing that we will be free one day. This will be the day when all of God's children will be able to sing with new meaning—"my country 'tis of thee; sweet land of liberty; of thee I sing; land where my fathers died, land of the pilgrim's pride; from every mountain side, let freedom ring"—and if America is to be a great nation, this must become true.

So let freedom ring from the prodigious hilltops of New Hampshire.

Let freedom ring from the mighty mountains of New York.

Let freedom ring from the heightening Alleghenies of Pennsylvania.

Let freedom ring from the snow-capped Rockies of Colorado.

Let freedom ring from the curvaceous slopes of California.

But not only that.

Let freedom ring from Stone Mountain of Georgia.

Let freedom ring from Lookout Mountain of Tennessee.

Let freedom ring from every hill and molehill of Mississippi, from every mountainside, let freedom ring.

And when we allow freedom to ring, when we let it ring from every village and hamlet, from every state and city, we will be able to speed up that day when all of God's children—black men and white men, Jews and Gentiles, Catholics and Protestants—will be able to join hands and to sing in the words of the old Negro spiritual, "Free at last, free at last; thank God Almighty, we are free at last."

Excerpted from Martin Luther King Jr.'s, "I Have a Dream" speech. Copyright 1963 Martin Luther King Jr., renewed 1991 by Coretta Scott King. Reprinted by arrangement with The Heirs to the Estate of Martin Luther King Jr., c/o Writers House, Inc., as agent for the proprietor.

Document 11: The Civil Rights Act of 1964

In July 1964, Congress passed civil rights legislation first proposed by President John Kennedy in June 1963. This legislation, known as the Civil Rights Act of 1964, removed barriers that prevented blacks from voting and outlawed discrimination in restaurants, hotels, theaters, retail stores, and other public places. President Lyndon Johnson signed the bill into law on July 2, 1964.

TITLE I–VOTING RIGHTS

SEC. 101 (2). No person acting under color of law shall—

(A) in determining whether any individual is qualified under State law or laws to vote in any Federal election, apply any standard, practice, or procedure different from the standards, practices, or procedures applied under such law or laws to other individuals within the same county, parish, or similar political subdivision who have been found by State officials to be qualified to vote; . . .

(C) employ any literacy test as a qualification for voting in any Federal election unless (i) such test is administered to each individual wholly in writing; and (ii) a certified copy of the test and of the answers given by the individual is furnished to him within twenty-five days of the submission of his request made within the period of time during which records and papers are required to be retained and preserved pursuant to title III of the Civil Rights Act of 1960 . . .

TITLE II–INJUNCTIVE RELIEF AGAINST DISCRIMINATION IN PLACES OF PUBLIC ACCOMMODATION

SEC. 201. (a) All persons shall be entitled to the full and equal enjoyment of the goods, services, facilities, privileges, advantages, and accommodations of any place of public accommodation, as defined in this section, without discrimination or segregation on the ground of race, color, religion, or national origin.

(b) Each of the following establishments which serves the public is a place of public accommodation within the meaning of this title if its operations affect commerce, or if discrimination or segregation by it is supported by State action:

(1) any inn, motel, or other establishment which provides lodging to transient guests, other than an establishment located within a building which contains not more than five rooms for rent or hire and which is actually occupied by the proprietor of such establishment as his residence;

(2) any restaurant, cafeteria, lunch room, lunch counter, soda fountain, or other facility principally engaged in selling food for consumption on the premises . . .

(3) any motion picture house, theater, concert hall, sports arena, stadium or other place of exhibition or entertainment . . .

(d) Discrimination or segregation by an establishment is supported by State action within the meaning of this title if such discrimination or segregation (1) is carried on under color of any law, statute, ordinance, or regulation; or (2) is carried on under color of any custom or usage required or enforced by officials of the State or political subdivision thereof . . .

SEC. 202. All persons shall be entitled to be free, at any establishment or place, from discrimination or segregation of any kind on the ground of race, color, religion, or national origin, if such discrimination or segregation is or purports to be required by any law, statute, ordinance, regulation, rule, or order of a State or any agency or political subdivision thereof . . .

SEC. 206. (a) Whenever the Attorney General has reasonable cause to believe that any person or group of persons is engaged in a pattern or practice of resistance to the full enjoyment of any of the rights secured by this title, the Attorney General may bring a civil action in the appropriate district court of the United States by filing with it a complaint . . . requesting such preventive relief, including an application for a permanent or temporary injunction, restraining order or other order against the person or persons responsible for such pattern or practice, as he deems necessary to insure the full enjoyment of the rights herein described. . . .

TITLE VI–NONDISCRIMINATION IN FEDERALLY ASSISTED PROGRAMS

SEC. 601. No person in the United States shall, on the ground of race, color, or national origin, be excluded from participation in, be denied the benefits of, or be subjected to discrimination under any program or activity receiving Federal financial assistance.

Congressional Record, 1964.

CHRONOLOGY

1868
The Fourteenth Amendment to the U.S. Constitution is ratified. This amendment contains the "equal protection" clause, guaranteeing all U.S. citizens "equal protection of the laws."

1870
The Fifteenth Amendment to the Constitution is passed, stating that citizens of the United States cannot be denied the right to vote "on account of race, color, or previous condition of servitude."

1896
The U.S. Supreme Court decides the case of *Plessy v. Ferguson.* The Court upholds a Louisiana law mandating separate train cars for white and black passengers, ruling that laws separating the races "do not necessarily imply the inferiority of either race." This decision allows the states to enact segregation laws.

1909
W.E.B. Du Bois and other black intellectuals, meeting in New York City, form the National Association for the Advancement of Colored People (NAACP). The organization's goal is "to achieve, through peaceful and lawful means, equal citizenship rights for all American citizens by eliminating segregation in housing, employment, voting, schools, the courts, transportation, [and] recreation."

1936
Thurgood Marshall and other NAACP attorneys win a court decision that desegregates the University of Maryland School of Law.

1942
The Congress of Racial Equality (CORE) is formed at the University of Chicago.

April 1947
Jackie Robinson of the Brooklyn Dodgers becomes the first African American major league baseball player in the twentieth century.

July 26, 1948
President Harry Truman issues an executive order desegregating the U.S. armed forces.

May 17, 1954

The Supreme Court announces its decision in the case of *Brown v. Board of Education of Topeka, Kansas*. The Court outlaws racial segregation in public schools, ruling that segregated schools deprive black students of "the equal protection of the laws guaranteed by the Fourteenth Amendment."

December 1, 1955

Rosa Parks, a secretary of the Montgomery, Alabama, chapter of the NAACP, is arrested and fined for refusing to surrender her bus seat to a white passenger. Reverend Martin Luther King Jr. leads a year-long boycott of Montgomery's municipal buses, resulting in an end to segregated bus seating in Montgomery.

March 12, 1956

More than one hundred members of Congress from the South issue the "Southern Manifesto," condemning the *Brown v. Board of Education* decision.

January 11, 1957

Reverend King and other black clergymen form the Southern Christian Leadership Conference (SCLC) in Atlanta.

August 1957

Congress passes the Civil Rights Act of 1957, the first piece of civil rights legislation since the Reconstruction. This law establishes a civil rights division within the Justice Department.

September 1957

Governor Orval Faubus of Arkansas attempts to block the integration of Central High School in Little Rock. President Dwight Eisenhower sends the 101st Airborne Division to Little Rock to enforce a court order mandating the integration of Central High.

February 1960

Black college students in Greensboro, North Carolina, sit in at a Woolworth's lunch counter to protest the store's policy prohibiting black customers from being served. The sit-in movement spreads to Nashville, Atlanta, and other Southern cities, resulting in the desegregation of many eateries.

April 1960

The Student Nonviolent Coordinating Committee (SNCC) is formed by black students at a conference in Raleigh, North Carolina.

May 1960
Congress passes the Civil Rights Act of 1960, extending the powers of the Civil Rights Commission and effecting stiff penalties for the firebombing of buildings.

Spring 1961
CORE and SNCC sponsor a series of "freedom rides" to desegregate Southern bus terminals. Freedom riders are met with opposition from hostile whites and police. One bus is burned.

November 1961
King and other civil rights leaders form the Albany Movement, a series of protests designed to end segregation in Albany, Georgia. The nine-month effort ends with few significant accomplishments.

September 1962
The Ku Klux Klan dynamites four black churches in Georgia.

James Meredith, a black air force veteran, is denied admission to the University of Mississippi in violation of a federal court order. Local residents and students riot on campus, causing two deaths. President John Kennedy federalizes the Mississippi National Guard to establish order and pressures Governor Ross Barnett to admit Meredith. Meredith enrolls and attends classes under the protection of federal marshals.

April 1963
King leads a campaign to desegregate Birmingham, Alabama. He is arrested and writes from his jail cell "Letter from a Birmingham Jail," a key document of the civil rights movement.

May 10, 1963
The Birmingham protests end when the city agrees to desegregate lunch counters, public drinking fountains, and public restrooms.

June 1963
Two black students integrate the University of Alabama, despite resistance led by Governor George Wallace.

June 11, 1963
President Kennedy delivers a nationally televised speech announcing his decision to ask Congress to pass legislation outlawing segregation in restaurants, hotels, and other social gathering places.

June 12, 1963
Medgar Evers, an NAACP field secretary, is murdered near his home in Jackson, Mississippi.

August 28, 1963

More than 250,000 protesters gather at the Lincoln Memorial in Washington, D.C., for the March on Washington for Jobs and Freedom. Martin Luther King Jr. delivers his "I Have a Dream" speech.

September 15, 1963

A bomb explodes in a Baptist church in Birmingham, Alabama, killing four young African American girls attending a Sunday school program.

November 27, 1963

Five days after President Kennedy's assassination, President Lyndon Johnson encourages Congress to pass Kennedy's proposed civil rights bill.

June 1964

The slain bodies of three civil rights workers are found near Philadelphia, Mississippi.

July 2, 1964

President Johnson signs into law the Civil Rights Act of 1964, outlawing segregation in restaurants, hotels, theaters, sports arenas, and other public places and creating the Equal Employment and Opportunity Commission to root out employment discrimination.

December 10, 1964

King wins the Nobel Peace Prize for his efforts in eliminating racial discrimination in the United States.

February 21, 1965

Malcolm X, a Black Muslim spokesman, is assassinated in Harlem.

March 21–25, 1965

King leads the Selma-to-Montgomery march to demand voting rights for Alabama's black citizens.

August 6, 1965

President Johnson signs into law the Voting Rights Act, eliminating barriers that prevent African American citizens from voting.

August 11–16, 1965

A race riot occurs in the Watts section of Los Angeles, leaving thirty-four dead and causing millions of dollars in property damage.

October 1966

The Black Panther Party is formed in Oakland, California. Its manifesto demands "power to determine the destiny of our Black Community."

June 1967

President Johnson nominates Thurgood Marshall to be the first African American justice of the U.S. Supreme Court.

Summer 1967

Major race riots occur in Newark, New Jersey, and Detroit, Michigan, causing fifty-six deaths and millions of dollars in property damage. Smaller-scale racial uprisings occur in Chicago, Cleveland, Milwaukee, and other Northern cities.

April 4, 1968

King is murdered in Memphis, Tennessee, where he had been supporting a strike by sanitation workers.

July 26, 1990

President George Bush signs into law the Americans with Disabilities Act, outlawing discrimination based on physical or mental handicap in employment, public accommodations, and transportation.

April 1992

A major race riot erupts in Los Angeles when four white policemen are acquitted of using excessive force against Rodney King, an African American motorist detained by police.

FOR FURTHER READING

Ralph Abernathy, *And the Walls Came Tumbling Down.* New York: Harper and Row, 1989. The story of the civil rights movement, as told by Martin Luther King Jr.'s closest associate.

Clayborne Carson, *In Struggle: SNCC and the Black Awakening of the 1960s.* New York: Viking Press, 1981. A study of the Student Nonviolent Coordinating Committee's role in the civil rights movement.

James Farmer, *Lay Bare the Heart: An Autobiography of the Civil Rights Movement.* New York: Arbor House, 1985. The autobiography of the founder of the Congress of Racial Equality.

Langston Hughes, *Fight for Freedom: The Story of the NAACP.* New York: W.W. Norton, 1962. A history of the National Association for the Advancement of Colored People, by one of the greatest African American poets.

Martin Luther King Jr., *Stride Toward Freedom: The Montgomery Story.* New York: Harper and Row, 1958. King tells the story of the Montgomery bus boycott.

Richard Kluger, *Simple Justice: The History of* Brown v. Board of Education *and Black America's Struggle for Equality.* New York: Alfred A. Knopf, 1976. A detailed history of the Supreme Court decision that desegregated public schools.

Malcolm X, *Malcolm X Speaks.* New York: Grove Press and Merit Publishing, 1965. The Black Muslim spokesman comments on a variety of racial issues.

August Meier and Elliott Rudwick, *CORE: A Study of the Civil Rights Movement, 1942–1968.* New York: Oxford University Press, 1973. A history of the civil rights movement focusing on the activities of the Congress of Racial Equality.

James Meredith, *Three Years in Mississippi.* Bloomington: Indiana University Press, 1966. Meredith's own story of his integration of the University of Mississippi.

Stephen B. Oates, *Let the Trumpet Sound: The Life of Martin Luther King, Jr.* New York: Harper and Row, 1982. A highly readable biography of King.

James Tackach, *Brown v. Board of Education*. San Diego: Lucent Books, 1998. A succinct history of the Supreme Court case that ended public school segregation, suitable for young adult readers.

Juan Williams, *Eyes on the Prize: America's Civil Rights Years, 1954–1965*. New York: Viking Books, 1987. A companion volume to the critically acclaimed PBS television documentary on the civil rights movement.

WORKS CONSULTED

James Baldwin, *The Fire Next Time*. New York: Vintage Books, 1962. An extended essay on the state of racial affairs in the United States by one of the foremost spokesmen of the civil rights movement.

————, *Nobody Knows My Name*. New York: Vintage Books, 1961. A collection of essays by Baldwin written after a tour of the South in the late 1950s.

————, *Notes of a Native Son*. Boston: Beacon Press, 1955. A collection of essays on racial and other issues by the eloquent African American essayist from Harlem.

Taylor Branch, *Parting the Waters: America in the King Years 1954–63*. New York: Simon and Schuster, 1988. A Pulitzer Prize–winning history of the civil rights movement, commencing with the *Brown v. Board of Education* case and concluding with the assassination of President John Kennedy.

Clayborne Carson et al., eds., *The Eyes on the Prize Civil Rights Reader*. New York: Penguin Books, 1991. A collection of key documents on the civil rights movement.

Abraham Chapman, ed., *New Black Voices: An Anthology of Contemporary Afro-American Literature*. New York: Mentor Books, 1972. A collection of works by key African American writers of the 1960s.

W.E.B. Du Bois, *The Souls of Black Folk*. New York: Penguin Books, 1989. This analysis of America's racial landscape was first published in 1903.

William Dudley, ed., *The Civil Rights Movement: Opposing Viewpoints*. San Diego: Greenhaven Press, 1996. A collection of speeches, articles, and other writings by supporters and opponents of the civil rights movement.

John Egerton, *Speak Now Against the Day: The Generation Before the Civil Rights Movement in the South*. New York: Alfred A. Knopf, 1995. A chronicle of events leading to the civil rights movement, from the 1930s through the early 1950s.

David Halberstam, *The Fifties*. New York: Villard Books, 1993. A social history of the decade during which the civil rights movement began.

Henry Hampton and Steve Fayer, *Voices of Freedom: An Oral History of the Civil Rights Movement from the 1950s Through the 1980s*. New York: Bantam Books, 1990. First-person testimony from a score of participants in the civil rights movement.

Martin Luther King Jr., *I Have a Dream: Writings and Speeches That Changed the World*. San Francisco: HarperSanFrancisco, 1992. A collection of King's major speeches and writings, with an introduction and timeline of key events in King's lifetime.

Jonathan Kozol, *Savage Inequalities: Children in America's Schools*. New York: HarperPerennial, 1991. A critique of American education focusing on inner-city public schools.

Abraham Lincoln, *Selected Speeches and Writings*. New York: Vintage Books, 1992. A collection of Lincoln's major speeches and writings.

Malcolm X and Alex Haley, *The Autobiography of Malcolm X*. New York: Ballantine Books, 1964. The life story of one of the key spokesmen of the Black Muslims.

Otto H. Olsen, ed., *The Thin Disguise: Turning Point in Negro History*, Plessy v. Ferguson. New York: Humanities Press, 1967. A collection of documents pertaining to the *Plessy v. Ferguson* Supreme Court decision.

Harvard Sitkoff, *The Struggle for Black Equality 1954–1980*. New York: Hill and Wang, 1981. A succinct history of the civil rights movement beginning with the *Brown v. Board of Education* decision. This text is highly recommended for the young-adult reader.

Henry David Thoreau, *Civil Disobedience and Other Essays*. New York: Dover Books, 1993. A collection of essays by the mid-nineteenth-century transcendentalist philosopher whose ideas greatly influenced Martin Luther King Jr.

Booker T. Washington, *Up from Slavery*. New York: Bantam Books, 1970. The influential autobiography of an important African American spokesman of the late-eighteenth and early-nineteenth centuries, first published in 1901.

Sanford Wexler, *The Civil Rights Movement: An Eyewitness History*. New York: Facts On File, 1993. A highly readable history of the civil rights movement, with chronologies and eyewitness testimony from key players in the major events.

INDEX

Abernathy, Reverend Ralph, 63
affirmative action, 76
African Americans
  are treated as second-class citizens, 20, 31–32,
    52–53
    con, 26–27
    in an integrated society, 58
  are treated better than other Africans, 27
  calling for integration, 55, 57
  citizenship rights for freed, 6
  contrasted with Jews, 20
  military service by, 10
  need for patience by, 39
  progress made for, 27–28, 29–30, 36, 40
    through civil rights movement, 75–76
  separate state for, 17, 54–55, 60–61
  unemployment rate for, 76, 81
  whites not an ally of, 59–60
  see also segregation
Albany Movement of 1961–1962, 70
Americans with Disabilities Act (1990), 77
armed forces. *See* military
Atlantic Monthly (magazine), 27

Baldwin, James
  on goal of civil rights movement, 35
  on Harlem, 23–24
  on need for integration, 55
  on nonviolence, 65–66
Barnett, Ross, 14
Billings, Henry, 7–8
Black Muslims, 54–55
"Black Power," 17
black studies, 75
bombings, 68
boycotts. *See* bus boycotts
Bradley, Bill, 78
Brown, Ronald, 73
Brown v. Board of Education, 11–12, 21–22, 52, 74
  educational opportunities through, 27–28
bus boycotts, 12
  as morally justified, 32
  as nonviolent, 34, 63–64
Bush, George, 77

Carey, Gordon R., 33
Central High School (Little Rock, Arkansas), 14,
  42, 46
church bombing, 68
citizenship, 6
Civil Rights Act (1957), 13, 46
Civil Rights Act (1964), 16, 65, 74–75
civil rights movement
  accomplishments of, 75, 76
  began transformation of American society, 73
  dates in, 7
  early activists in, 8
  economic disparities after, 81–82
  end of, 17, 79–80
  failure to achieve goals of, 78, 82
  founded on nonviolence, 63
  future influence of, 18–19

as helping other minorities, 76–77
  liberating the nation as goal of, 35
  slow progress in, 8–9
  see also legislation; protests; segregation
civil unrest. *See* violence
colleges. *See* universities
Connor, Bull, 64
courts
  Thurgood Marshall's cases in, 9–10
  unequal treatment of African Americans in, 22
  whites acquitted by all-white juries in, 69–70
  see also U.S. Supreme Court

demonstrations. *See* protests
discrimination
  after constitutional changes, 6
  employment, 6
  housing, 6, 48, 81
  need for federal government action on, 48
  in the North, 23–24
  persistence of, 81
  right to protest against, 31–32
Douglass, Frederick, 8
Du Bois, W.E.B., 20–21
  essays by, 8
  on improvements made for African Americans,
    28

economics
  advances made for African Americans in, 76
  racial disparities in, 81–82
education
  gains made by civil rights movement in, 75
  increased opportunities for African Americans in,
    27–28
  see also segregation, school
Eisenhower, Dwight D., 42
  civil rights legislation under, 46
  on school segregation, 14, 42
employment, 6
"equal protection of the law," 22, 54
Evers, Medgar, 68–69

Farmer, James, 53, 54, 63
Faubus, Orval, 42, 46, 47
Fire Next Time, The (Baldwin), 65–66
Forrest, Nathan Bedford, 7
freedom rides
  civil unrest through, 37–38
  white violence in, 68

Galamison, Milton, 55
government, U.S.
  interfering in South's racial matters, 41
  need for action by, 47–49
  need for legislation by, 46, 48
  should make civil rights decisions, 45
  vs. state/local government decisions, 41–44

Halberstam, David, 74
Harvard Business Review (magazine), 81
housing, 6, 48, 81

109

About the Author

James Tackach is the author of *Brown v. Board of Education, The Trial of John Brown, The Emancipation Proclamation,* and other books for young adults. He has also authored *Historic Homes of America* and *Great American Hotels*. His articles have appeared in the *New York Times, Providence Journal, America's Civil War*, and a variety of academic publications. Dr. Tackach teaches in the English department at Roger Williams University in Bristol, Rhode Island, and lives in Narragansett, Rhode Island.